"JESUS ONLY" CHURCHES

Zondervan
Guide to Cults &
Religious Movements

Titles in the series released in 1995

Unmasking the Cults   *by Alan W. Gomes*
Jehovah's Witnesses   *by Robert M. Bowman, Jr.*
Masonic Lodge   *by George A. Mather and Larry A. Nichols*
Mormonism   *by Kurt Van Gorden*
New Age Movement   *by Ron Rhodes*
Satanism   *by Bob and Gretchen Passantino*
Unification Church   *by J. Isamu Yamamoto*
Mind Sciences   *by Todd Ehrenborg*

Titles in the series released in 1998

Astrology and Psychic Phenomena   *by André Kole and Terry Holley*
Buddhism, Taoism and Other Far Eastern Religions
    by J. Isamu Yamamoto
Goddess Worship, Witchcraft and Neo-Paganism   *by Craig S. Hawkins*
"Jesus Only" Churches   *by E. Calvin Beisner*
Hinduism, TM and Hare Krishna   *by J. Isamu Yamamoto*
Unitarian Universalism   *by Alan W. Gomes*
Truth and Error: Comparative Charts of Cults and Christianity
    by Alan W. Gomes

ZONDERVAN
GUIDE to CULTS &
RELIGIOUS
MOVEMENTS

"JESUS ONLY" CHURCHES

E. CALVIN BEISNER

Author

Alan W. Gomes
Series Editor

ZondervanPublishingHouse
Grand Rapids, Michigan

A Division of HarperCollins*Publishers*

Dedicated to Arthur John Calvin Beisner

"Jesus Only" Churches
Copyright © 1998 by E. Calvin Beisner

Requests for information should be addressed to:
Zondervan Publishing House
Grand Rapids, Michigan 49530

Library of Congress Cataloging-in-Publication Data

Beisner, E. Calvin.
    "Jesus only" churches / E. Calvin Beisner.
        p.   cm. — (Zondervan guide to cults & religious movements)
    Includes bibliographical references.
    ISBN: 0-310-48871-0 (pbk.)
    1. Oneness Pentecostal churches — Controversial literature. 2. Pentecostal
churches — Controversial literature. I. Title. II. Series.
    BX8763.B45 1998
    289.9'4 — dc20   96-21589
                                                                                            CIP

Interior design by Art Jacobs

Printed in the United States of America

98 99 00 01 02 03 04 /❖ DP/ 10 9 8 7 6 5 4 3 2 1

 # Contents

How to Use This Book

The *Zondervan Guide to Cults and Religious Movements* comprises fifteen volumes, treating many of the most important groups and belief systems confronting the Christian church today. This series distills the most important facts about each and presents a well-reasoned, cogent Christian response. The authors in this series are highly qualified, well-respected professional Christian apologists with considerable expertise on their topics.

We have designed the structure and layout to help you find the information you need as quickly as possible. All the volumes are written in outline form, which allows us to pack substantial content into a short book. With some exceptions, each book contains, first, an introduction to the cult, movement, or belief system. The introduction gives a brief history of the group, its organizational structure, and vital statistics such as membership. Second, the theology section is arranged by doctrinal topic, such as God, Christ, sin, and salvation. The movement's position is set forth objectively, primarily from its own official writings. The group's teachings are then refuted point by point, followed by an affirmative presentation of what the Bible says about the doctrine. The third section is a discussion of witnessing tips. While each witnessing encounter must be handled individually and sensitively, this section provides some helpful general guidelines, including both dos and don'ts. The fourth section contains annotated bibliographies, listing works by the groups themselves and books written by Christians in response. Fifth, each book has a parallel comparison chart, with direct quotations from the group's literature in the left column and the biblical refutation on the right. Some of the books conclude with a glossary.

One potential problem with a detailed outline is that it is easy to lose one's place in the overall structure. Therefore, we have provided graphical "signposts" at the top of the odd-numbered pages. Functioning like a "you are here" map in a shopping mall, these graphics show your place in the outline, including the sections that come before and after your current position. (Those familiar with modern computer software will note immediately the resemblance to a "drop-down" menu bar, where the second-level choices vary depending on the currently selected main menu item.) In the theology section we have also used "icons" in the margins to make clear at a glance whether the material is being presented from the group's viewpoint or the Christian viewpoint. For example, in the Mormonism volume the sections presenting the Mormon position are indicated with a picture resembling the angel Moroni in the margin; the biblical view is shown by a drawing of the Bible.

We hope you will find these books useful as you seek "to give an answer to everyone who asks you to give the reason for the hope that you have" (1 Peter 3:15).

— Alan W. Gomes, Ph.D.
Series Editor

 # Part I: Introduction

I. Historical Background

A. *Oneness ("Jesus Only") Pentecostals: Offshoot from Early Pentecostalism*
1. Oneness Pentecostalism's roots are in the North American Pentecostal movement of the early 1900s. It emerged from the Assemblies of God (AG) in 1914.
2. From 1913 to 1916, several Pentecostal leaders, including R. E. McAlister, Frank J. Ewart, Glenn A. Cook, and Garfield T. Haywood, began teaching that the baptismal formula must be "in the name of the Lord Jesus Christ," not "in the name of the Father, and of the Son, and of the Holy Spirit."
3. Prompted by J. Roswell Flower's opposition to Oneness theology and baptismal formula, the AG, in its Third General Council (1915), opposed Oneness teaching.
4. In its Fourth General Council (1916), the AG adopted a "Statement of Fundamental Truths" that forcefully maintained the Trinity, effectively banning 156 of the AG's 585 ministers.
5. Since then, Oneness Pentecostalism has been distinguished by its Christology (doctrine of Christ), theology (doctrine of God), and soteriology (doctrine of salvation).

B. *The Rise of Oneness Organizations*
1. On January 3, 1916, several Oneness ministers barred by the AG's "Statement of Fundamental Truths," including Howard A. Goss, H. G. Rodgers, and D. C. O. Opperman, formed the General Assembly of Apostolic Assemblies (GAAA).
2. GAAA merged in January 1918 with the Pentecostal Assemblies of the World (PAW), a loose-knit and largely black fellowship begun in Los Angeles in 1906, adopting PAW's name and charter.
3. Racial tensions in the early 1920s led to schisms. Two offshoots, which involved the majority of white pastors, formed:
   a. Emmanuel's Church in Jesus Christ (ECJC), based in Oklahoma, Texas, and Louisiana, and a loose-knit group from the St. Louis area, which merged in 1927 to form the Apostolic Church of Jesus Christ (ACJC);
   b. the Pentecostal Ministerial Alliance (PMA), which formed in Jackson, Tennessee, in 1925 and adopted the new name Pentecostal Church, Incorporated (PCI), in 1932.

7

4. Many other small Oneness organizations formed by schism in the 1920s.

5. In November 1931, ACJC and PAW merged as the Pentecostal Assemblies of Jesus Christ (PAJC).

6. Racial tensions resulted in most of PAJC's ministers reviving PAW as a separate organization in 1937.

7. In 1945, PCI and the remaining, mostly white, ministers in PAJC merged as the United Pentecostal Church (UPC), which, beginning with 1,800 ministers and over 900 churches, has become the largest and, through aggressive evangelism and publishing efforts, most influential Oneness organization. Now called the United Pentecostal Church, International (UPCI; it added *International* to its name in 1972), this group will be our focus due to its dominance among Oneness groups.

C. *Recent Schisms in the United Pentecostal Church, International*

1. UPCI pastor L. H. Hardwick split from the denomination in 1986, protesting increasing control by people he called "legalists." Taking his 3,000-member Christ Church, in Nashville, Tennessee, with him, Hardwick formed Global Christian Ministries, a Oneness ministerial alliance that has been joined by several hundred former UPCI pastors.

2. Following a vote by UPCI leaders in October 1992 to require all affiliated pastors to pledge conformity with the UPCI's "Holiness Standard"—promising to refrain, particularly, from watching television, wearing immodest clothing, and participating in "worldly sports and amusements"—over 200 pastors left the denomination and formed the International Network of Ministers (INM). UPCI pastor Richard Gazowsky, of the Voice of Pentecost Church in San Francisco, predicted in the spring of 1993 that 800 ministers would leave the denomination soon. It is not yet disclosed how many defected.[1]

II. Vital Statistics

A. *Oneness Pentecostalism as a Whole*

1. Oneness Pentecostalism worldwide comprises about 90 denominations in 57 countries.

2. Estimated affiliated church members worldwide in 1990 totaled about 1.4 million (0.8 percent of all Pentecostals and 0.09 percent of all members of Christian churches worldwide), of whom about 75 percent (1.03 million) were affiliated with the UPCI.[2]

---

[1]Lee Grady, "Dispute Causes Upheaval in UPC," *Charisma* (May 1933): 76–77.

[2]Because many Oneness Pentecostal denominations are loosely knit and keep few membership statistics, aggregate membership statistics for Oneness Pentecostalism are gross estimates with wide margins of error and ranges of confidence. Data for the UPCI, the denomination focused on in this book, are more reliable, except for projections of the effect of the 1993 schism.

3. The vast majority of Pentecostals, both worldwide and in every major geographical region, are Trinitarian, not Oneness.

4. Oneness Pentecostalism is strongest in the United States, Canada, South Asia, and Oceania.

5. Oneness Pentecostalism is expected to grow worldwide to about 1,513,000 members by A.D. 2000, at which time it is anticipated to constitute about 0.67 percent of all Pentecostals and about 0.09 percent of all professing Christians worldwide.[3]

B. United Pentecostal Church International[4]

1. Membership Figures

   The schism of 1993 throws membership figures into doubt from that year forward. Before the schism, worldwide membership was about 1.1 million. About two years later, it decreased to about 1.02 million.

2. Divisions and Their Responsibilities

   a. Editorial: Produces literature and tracts, especially for evangelism.

   b. Pentecostal Publishing House: Spreads the gospel through literature. Under the control of the Executive Board, it publishes under the name Word Aflame Press. Over one hundred titles are in print, with several more added each year.

   c. Education: Exercises jurisdiction over all endorsed Bible colleges: Apostolic Bible Institute, Apostolic Missionary Institute, Christian Life College, Gateway College of Evangelism, Indiana Bible College, Jackson College of Ministries, Kent Christian College, Texas Bible College, and United Pentecostal Bible Institute. It also provides structure for an association of UPCI schools.

   d. Foreign Missions

   e. Home Missions: Responsible for church planting, metro evangelism, Spanish evangelism, black evangelism, prison ministry (Christian Prisoner Fellowship), deaf ministry, Indian ministry, and ethnic ministry.

   f. Harvestime: Produces a radio program.

   g. Youth

   h. Sunday School[5]

C. The Pentecostal Publishing House

1. Publishes books and audio tapes as Word Aflame Press. The 1992–93 catalog listed 10 new releases (all books) and nearly 150 backlist books and tapes (or tape series).

---

[3]Statistical data on Oneness Pentecostalism, the broader Pentecostal movement, and general Christianity derive from David B. Barrett, "Statistics, Global," in *Dictionary of Pentecostal and Charismatic Movements,* ed. Stanley M. Burgess, Gary B. McGee, and Patrick H. Alexander (Grand Rapids: Zondervan, 1988), 810–30.

[4]Founded 1945; headquarters, Hazelwood, Missouri, near St. Louis.

[5]David Bernard, C. A. Brewer, and P. D. Buford, *Meet the United Pentecostal Church International* (Hazelwood, Mo.: Word Aflame Press, 1989), 119–31.

2. Publishes Sunday school materials as Word Aflame Publications. The 1992–93 catalog listed approximately thirty-five items.
3. Publishes tracts under their own name. The 1992–93 catalog listed forty tracts.

D. *Other Oneness Pentecostal Denominations*

1. Apostolic Overcoming Holy Church of God (1917), headquartered in Birmingham, Alabama: mostly black, 13,000 members in 197 churches (1987). (Founding and data collection dates appear in parentheses.)
2. Assemblies of the Lord Jesus Christ (1952 merger of Assemblies of Jesus Christ, Church of the Lord Jesus Christ, and Jesus Only Apostolic Church of God), headquartered in Memphis, Tennessee: racially integrated, 20,000 members, 400 ministers, 300 churches in 22 states and 6 foreign countries (1987)
3. Bible Way Churches of Our Lord Jesus Christ Worldwide (1957), headquartered in Washington, D.C.: 30,000 members in 350 congregations in U.S., 1,000 members in 16 congregations in U.K. (claimed, 1975)
4. Church of the Lord Jesus Christ of the Apostolic Faith (1919, reorganized 1935), headquartered in Philadelphia: mainly black, 7,000 members, 92 churches (n.d.)
5. Pentecostal Assemblies of the World (1907; merged in 1918 with the General Assembly of Apostolic Assemblies [schism from Assemblies of God]), headquartered in Indianapolis, Indiana: predominantly black but purposely interracial in membership and leadership, claims 500,000 members worldwide in 1,400 churches in all 50 states and 1,400 churches in Africa, Asia, Europe, and the West Indies (1987)
6. Pentecostal Churches of the Apostolic Faith Association (1957; schism from Pentecostal Assemblies of the World), headquartered in Louisville, Kentucky: 50,000 adherents in 125 churches with 400 ministers (1987)

 # Part II: *Theology*

I. Christology: Is Christ Divided?

A. *Basic Statement of the Oneness Position*

1. In general, Oneness writers teach that Jesus Christ is God;
2. Jesus is the Father and the Holy Spirit, so in the incarnation "all of God" became incarnate; and
3. Jesus is the Son (not only "of Man" but also "of God") only in his incarnation.

B. *Arguments Used by Oneness Writers to Support Their Christology*

1. Jesus Christ is God.

   a. A variety of Bible verses prove that Jesus is God, including John 20:28; Romans 9:5; Philippians 2:5–6; Titus 2:13; 2 Peter 1:1; and 1 John 5:20.[1]

   b. To say that Jesus is God does not mean that he is God the Son. Oneness theology reserves the title *Son of God* only for the incarnate Christ.

2. The "fullness of the Deity" can dwell bodily in Jesus (Col. 2:9) only if he is the Father and the Holy Spirit.

   a. For arguments that Jesus is the Father and the Holy Spirit, see II.B.1.e.

   b. David K. Bernard, the UPCI's most prolific writer on theology and, particularly, on Oneness versus the Trinity,[2] and an associate editor in UPCI's Editorial Division, argues against the Trinity: "If there were several persons in the Godhead, according to Colossians 2:9 they would all be resident in the bodily form of Jesus."[3]

3. For Jesus, sonship (whether of God or of man) is not eternal but a temporary role with beginning and end.

   a. "The Sonship began at Bethlehem. The Incarnation was the time when the Sonship began.... Here [in Luke 1:35] it is clearly revealed that the humanity of the Lord Jesus is the Son."[4]

---

[1]See, e.g., David K. Bernard, *The Oneness of God* (Hazelwood, Mo.: Word Aflame Press, 1983), 55–58.

[2]The 1992–1993 Pentecostal Publishing House catalog lists fifteen books and three audio tape series by Bernard, all on doctrinal subjects, with five of the books specifically on the doctrine of Oneness. The catalog lists no other author with nearly so many books on any subject, let alone on these specific subjects.

[3]Bernard, *Oneness of God,* 57; see also p. 216.

[4]Gordon Magee, *Is Jesus in the Godhead or Is The Godhead in Jesus?* (Hazelwood, Mo.: Word Aflame Press, 1988), 32.

b. " ... the verses of Scripture that speak of creation by the Son cannot mean the Son existed substantially at creation as a person apart from the Father. The Old Testament proclaims that one individual Being created us, and He is Jehovah, the Father ... [Malachi 2:10; Isaiah 44:24]."[5]

c. "The Word had pre-existence and the Word was God (the Father), so we can use [the title *Word*] without reference to humanity. However, the Son always refers to the Incarnation and we cannot use it in the absence of the human element."[6]

d. "The word *begotten* is a form of the verb *beget,* which means 'to procreate, to father, to sire.' Thus *begotten* indicates a definite point in time, the point at which conception takes place. ... So, the very words *begotten* and *Son* each contradict the word *eternal* as applied to the Son of God."[7]

e. "Not only did the Sonship have a beginning, but it will ... [also] have an ending" (see 1 Cor. 15:23–28).

  (1) " ... verse [28] is impossible to explain if one thinks of a 'God the Son' who is co-equal and co-eternal with God the Father.

  (2) "But it is easily explained if we realize that 'Son of God' refers to a specific role that God temporarily assumed for the purpose of redemption."[8]

f. "The term 'eternal Son' is never found in the Bible, and thank God it is not!

  (1) "If it was, it would teach Jesus as Son forever, praying, learning, being lesser, 'not knowing,' and so on. For all these things are in the Scripture associated with the Son.

  (2) "Indeed, the Bible flatly and plainly contradicts the 'eternal Son' idea in John 3:16 and everywhere it mentions the 'begotten Son.' The words *eternal* and *begotten* are contradictory and mean completely opposite things."[9]

4. Bible verses that appear to reveal distinctions between Jesus and the Father or the Holy Spirit actually reveal distinctions solely between the divine and human natures of the incarnate Jesus.

  a. "When we see a plural (especially a duality) used in reference to Jesus, we must think of the humanity and deity of Jesus Christ. There is a real duality, but it is a distinction between Spirit and flesh, not a distinction of persons in God. ... When we see a plural

---

[5]Bernard, *Oneness of God,* 117.
[6]Ibid., 103.
[7]Ibid., 103–4.
[8]Ibid., 106.
[9]Magee, *Is Jesus,* 25.

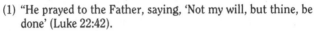

in relation to God, we must view it as a plurality of roles or relationships to mankind, not a plurality of persons."[10]

b. "The death of Jesus is a particularly good example. His divine Spirit did not die, but His human body did. We cannot say that God died, so we cannot say 'God the Son' died. On the other hand, we can say that the Son of God died because Son refers to humanity."[11]

c. "The Bible does indicate that Jesus had a human will as well as the divine will.

(1) "He prayed to the Father, saying, 'Not my will, but thine, be done' (Luke 22:42).

(2) "John 6:38 shows the existence of two wills: He came not to do His own will (human will), but to do the Father's will (the divine will)."[12]

(3) "Most problems in people's minds concerning the Godhead come from this great mystery. They cannot understand the dual nature of Christ and cannot correctly separate his two roles."[13]

d. "When Jesus said, 'I and my Father are one,' He spoke as God. When He said, 'My God, my God, why hast thou forsaken me?' He spoke as a man. He was man in a genuine sense, even to the extent of being able to feel God-forsaken under certain circumstances. The dual nature of the Lord Jesus Christ explains and even harmonizes what on the surface seems to be a contradiction."[14]

C. Refutation of Oneness Arguments on Christology

1. Summary Comparison: Historic, Biblical Christianity

a. Agrees that Jesus Christ is fully God,

b. Denies that he is either God the Father or the Holy Spirit, and

c. Denies that he is the Son of God only in his incarnation, teaching instead that

(1) he has been distinct from the Father and the Spirit as the Son of God for eternity, and

(2) he became Son of Man at his incarnation.

2. Jesus is God

Trinitarianism agrees and uses many of the same arguments to support it.

3. "All the fullness of the Deity" can dwell in Christ "in bodily form" (Col. 2:9) without equating Jesus with the Father and the Holy Spirit.

---

[10]Bernard, *Oneness of God,* 171.
[11]Ibid., 99–100.
[12]Ibid., 93.
[13]Ibid., 64.
[14]Magee, *Is Jesus,* 16.

13

a. For refutation of Oneness arguments that Jesus is the Father and the Holy Spirit, see II.C.1.e.

b. Bernard's argument against Trinitarian Christology that "Jesus is not just a part of God, but *all* of God is resident in Him" attacks a straw man, since Trinitarianism acknowledges that "in Christ all the fullness of the Deity lives in bodily form" (Col. 2:9).

4. Though his human sonship had a beginning, Jesus' divine sonship is not a mere temporary role with beginning and end. His sonship is eternal and the term *Son* properly applies to the preincarnate Word.

a. Luke 1:35 applies not to the divine but to the human nature of Christ and therefore says nothing of whether his divine sonship is eternal.

b. Bernard argues that since Jehovah alone created the world, the Son of God cannot have created it. But this begs the question by presupposing that if both the Father and the Son are God yet distinct persons, they must be two Gods.

   (1) But the doctrine of the Trinity says that Father, Son, and Holy Spirit, though distinct persons, are one and the same God, Jehovah.

   (2) Therefore, if the doctrine of the Trinity is true, then even though three distinct persons, Father (1 Cor. 8:6a; Heb. 1:2), Son (Col. 1:15–16), and Holy Spirit (Gen. 1:1–2), created the world, nonetheless one God, Jehovah, created it.

c. Bernard's assertion that the term *Son* "always refers to the Incarnation and we cannot use it in the absence of the human element" begs the question; merely asserting it does not prove it.

d. Biblical passages that speak of the Son as "begotten" or "only begotten" do not argue against his eternality as the Son.

   (1) The Son's having been begotten (from Greek *gennáō*) relates to his conception in the womb of Mary nine months before birth (Matt. 1:20; Luke 1:31, 35[?]; 2:21), his birth from Mary (Matt. 2:1–2, 4; Luke 1:35[?]; 2:11), and his resurrection (Acts 13:33; probably Heb. 1:5 and 5:5).[15] If having been "begotten" at birth and resurrection does not prevent his existence as the Son before both, having been "begotten" in conception does not prevent his existence as the Son before his conception.

   (2) The word sometimes translated "only begotten" (Gk. *monogenēs*) derives not from *only* (Gk. *monos*) and *beget* or *give birth* (Gk. *gennáō*), a combination that would yield *monógonos* or *monogénnētos*, but from *only* and *kind* (Gk. *génos*),

---

[15]The contexts of Heb. 1:5 and 5:5 make it probable that in these instances the phrase "today I have begotten you" (NIV note) refers not to Christ's incarnation but to his resurrection. If so, then this phrase never refers to his incarnation.

and its meaning is not properly "only begotten" but "unique," "one of a kind," "the only member of a kin or kind," "single."[16]

(3) Bernard claims that "the very words *begotten* and *Son* each contradict the word *eternal* as applied to the Son of God." But this implies that one cannot use the word *eternal* as applied to the Father either, for without an offspring one is not a father. Yet Bernard elsewhere insists that the title "everlasting [eternal] Father" (Isa. 9:6) designates Christ as God the Father.[17]

e. From 1 Corinthians 15:23–28 Bernard maintains that Christ's sonship will come to an end since the Son will be subject (*hypotagēsetai,* from *hypotássoō*) to the Father. This argument fails because:

(1) It presupposes that submission proves inferiority of nature, yet: (a) wives are not inferior by nature to their husbands yet are to be subject (*hypotassómenoi*) to them (Eph. 5:21–22); (b) citizens are not inferior by nature to their governors yet are to be subject (*hypotássesthe*) to them (Rom. 13:1); and (c) Jesus was not inferior by nature to Joseph and Mary yet was subject (*hypotassómenos*) to them (Luke 2:51).

(2) It neglects that the passage predicts *continuing* subjection of the Son to the Father, a continuing distinction between them.

f. Magee's argument that if Jesus were eternally the Son of God he would be eternally "praying, learning, being lesser, 'not knowing,'" fails:

(1) Because it does not distinguish between the attributes of Jesus' *human* (dependence, humiliation, limitation) and *divine* (self-existence, glory, infinity) natures; and

(2) Because it misunderstands the biblical use of *beget* related to the Son.

5. Oneness theology wrongly describes all distinctions between Father (or Holy Spirit) and Son as between Jesus' divine and human natures.

a. Bernard's interpretive principles about plurals in reference to Jesus and God are mistaken.

---

[16]Walter Bauer, *A Greek-English Lexicon of the New Testament and Other Early Christian Literature,* trans. William F. Arndt and F. Wilbur Gingrich, rev. F. Wilbur Gingrich and Frederick W. Danker, 2d ed. (Chicago: University of Chicago Press, 1979), 527; Henry G. Liddell and Robert Scott, comps., *A Greek-English Lexicon,* rev. Henry S. Jones and Roderick McKenzie et al., 9th ed. (Oxford: Oxford University Press, 1940), 1144; James H. Moulton and George Milligan, *The Vocabulary of the Greek New Testament* (reprint, Grand Rapids: Eerdmans, 1976), 417. As Bartels observes, "Lit[erally *monogenēs*] means 'of a single kind', and could even be used in this sense of the Phoenix (1 Clem[ent] 25:2). It is only distantly related to *gennaō,* beget. The idea of 'only begotten' goes back to Jerome who used *unigenitus* in the [Latin] Vulg[ate] to counter the Arian claim that Jesus was not begotten but made. *[M]onogenēs* reflects the Heb[rew] *yāḥîd* of Isaac (Gen. 22:2, 12, 16) of whom it is used in Heb. 11:16" (Karl-Heinz Bartels, "One," in *The New International Dictionary of New Testament Theology,* ed. Colin Brown, 4 vols. [Grand Rapids: Zondervan, 1975–85], 2:725; hereafter abbreviated as *NIDNTT*).

[17]Bernard, *Oneness of God,* 66.

(1) They impose his prior theological commitment on Scripture rather than allowing Scripture to determine his theology.

(2) When he insists that the duality seen in cases like Jesus' prayers (e.g., John 17:10–11, 25–26) "is a distinction between Spirit and flesh," that is, between the divine and human natures of Christ, "not a distinction of persons in God," he not only identifies Jesus, in his divine nature, with the Father, but also either

(a) Implies that Jesus was not fully man by making his divine Spirit substitute for the human spirit as the animating principle in the body, thus depriving the human side of Christ of that element of humanity;[18] or else

(b) Implies that Jesus was two persons by enabling each to talk to the other using first person (I, me, my, mine) and second person (you, your) pronouns.[19]

(c) And both of these mutually exclusive errors imply a sub-biblical view of the atoning sacrifice of Christ, for either (i) the sacrifice was not made by a proper representative of man, or else (ii) the sacrifice was made only by a man and therefore was not sufficient to pay the infinite debt of sin.

b. By denying that Christ died for men's sins *as God* (not merely as man), Oneness theology implies an atonement and redemption inadequate for man's salvation, for:[20]

(1) No other sacrifice would be adequate to pay the infinite debt for man's sin, for no other sacrifice would have been of infinite value. It is impossible for a mere human to make full atonement and ransom for sin; God must do it (Ps. 49:7–9, 15).

(2) Therefore it was essential that the one who died as a ransom and satisfaction for man's sin should be both human (to represent human beings properly; 1 Tim. 2:5; Rom. 5:12–19) and God.

(3) Any other redeemer would put people in debt and service to someone other than God, for we belong to whoever redeems us (1 Cor. 6:19–20; see also 7:22–23; Rev. 5:9).

---

[18]This view resembles Apollinarianism, a view rejected by the church at the Council of Constantinople in A.D. 381 because it denied Christ's perfect manhood (J. F. Bethune-Baker, *An Introduction to the Early History of Christian Doctrine to the Time of the Council of Chalcedon* [London: Methuen and Company, 1903], 239–54).

[19]This view is akin to Nestorianism, which represented the divine Logos as dwelling in the man Christ Jesus, so that the union between the two natures was somewhat analogous to the indwelling of the Spirit, a view condemned by the church at the Council of Chalcedon in A.D. 451 because it effectively denied the incarnation and thus the deity of Christ and the sufficiency of the atonement to pay for sin. See Bethune-Baker, *History*, 255–80.

[20]My argument here follows that of Anselm. See his *Cur Deus Homo?* in *A Scholastic Miscellany: Anselm to Ockham*, ed. Eugene R. Fairweather, Library of Christian Classics (Philadelphia: Westminster, 1956), I.xx, xxi, xxv, II.vi, vii; 136, 138–39, 145–46, 150–52.

c. Although historic orthodox teaching affirms that Christ had both a divine and a human will, Oneness Christology's understanding of two wills in Christ divides Christ into two persons.

   (1) Bernard rightly notes that "Jesus had a human will as well as the divine will," but when he explains Jesus' prayer, "not my will, but yours be done" (Luke 22:42), as from Jesus' human to his divine nature, he effectively splits Jesus into two persons.

   (2) To have a human will is not the same as being a person.

      (a) Before the Word became incarnate (became a person), he was already one person, and that person was divine.

      (b) After he became incarnate, he was still one person, and since he cannot change (Mal. 3:6; see also Heb. 13:8), he must have remained the same person he was before the incarnation.

      (c) Therefore the *person* of the incarnate Word must have been divine, not human.

      (d) Therefore Christ's human *nature* (to which the divine nature was united in the one *person* of Christ) must have possessed no personality *independent of the divine person* of the Word, though it did possess human intelligence, will, and passion.[21]

   (3) Only a person (self) can function as an agent, that is, a center or subject of intelligence, will, and passion, only a self can think, will, and feel.

   (4) But Bernard, by explaining the prayers of Jesus as prayers from his human nature to his divine nature (God the Father), attributes to the human nature of Jesus thinking, willing, and feeling distinct from the indwelling divine nature and person.

   (5) Therefore, although he denies it in theory, Bernard treats the human nature of Jesus as a distinct person from the divine person of Jesus.

   (6) Therefore, Bernard's explanation of the prayers of Jesus leads inexorably both to

      (a) Splitting Christ's person, contrary to 1 Corinthians 1:13; 8:6; Ephesians 4:5; and

      (b) Denying the real incarnation, for if the human person of Jesus was not identical to the divine person of Jesus, then the Word did not *become* flesh but merely *indwelt* flesh, contrary to John 1:14.

---

[21]That human *nature* does not include personality, although it does include intelligence, will, and passion (emotion), is clear from the fact that the whole human race has the properties of intelligence, will, and passion but is not itself a person, i.e., is not personal.

(7) Along with other Oneness thinkers, Bernard is confused about the incarnation. While he believes that "Most problems in people's minds concerning the Godhead come from this great mystery. They cannot understand the dual nature of Christ and cannot correctly separate his two roles,"[22] he misunderstands the biblical teaching of the uniting of two natures, divine and human, in the one divine person of Christ and therefore errs in three contrary directions:

    (a) Sometimes he writes of Christ and his activities as mere roles, pretenses: "Sometimes . . . the Bible describes Jesus . . . acting in both roles [human and divine] in the same story."[23]

    (b) Sometimes he writes of Christ's two natures as if they were distinct persons.

    (c) Sometimes he writes of Christ as if in him the divine Spirit substituted for the human spirit and so Christ was not fully human.

(8) By so dividing Christ as to make it possible for his human nature to speak to his divine nature and vice versa, Oneness theology denies the unity of Christ's person in practice, if not in theory, and therefore

    (a) Implies that either a mere man, not God, purchased us, which even if possible (contra Psalm 49:7–9, 15) would make us belong not to God but to that man, or that whoever paid our penalty was not a man and therefore not a proper representative for us (1 Tim. 2:5).

    (b) "Is Christ divided?" (1 Cor. 1:13). No.

    (c) Instead, Christ paid the penalty as a *man* (Matt. 20:28) and as *God* (Acts 20:28).

  d. If the Word (John 1:1) merely assumed a role, then he did not truly *become* flesh (John 1:14) or man (1 Tim. 2:5) but merely *acted as if* he did.

    (1) Bernard elsewhere affirms the real humanity of Christ, but that affirmation is logically incompatible with his description of the Son of God as a mere "role that God temporarily assumed for the purpose of redemption."[24]

    (2) Did God so love the world that he merely played a role, that the world through that role might be saved (John 3:16)?

    (3) Did a mere role love me and give its phony self for me (Gal. 2:20)?

---

[22]Bernard, *Oneness of God,* 64.
[23]Ibid., 88.
[24]Ibid., 106.

(4) Is this how we know what love is, that the Father pretended to be someone he was not and laid down the life he pretended to have (but did not) for us (1 John 3:16)?

D. Arguments Used to Prove Orthodox Christology to a Oneness Adherent

1. Basic Statement of Orthodox Christology

    a. Orthodox Christianity confesses, as in the Chalcedonian Creed (A.D. 451),[25]

    (1) "that the Son [of God] and our Lord Jesus Christ is to be confessed as one and the same [person],[26]

    (2) "that he is perfect in Godhead and also perfect in manhood; very God and very man,[27]

    (3) "of a reasonable soul and [human] body consisting;[28]

    (4) "consubstantial with the Father as touching his Godhead,[29]

    (5) "and consubstantial with us as touching his Manhood;[30]

    (6) "made in all things like unto us, sin only excepted;

    (7) "begotten of his Father before the worlds according to his Godhead;[31]

    (8) "but in these last days for us men and for our salvation born [into the world] of the Virgin Mary, the Mother of God according to his manhood.[32]

    (9) "This one and the same [Christ, Son, Lord, Only-begotten,][33]

---

[25]Except where noted, the text follows that of Philip Schaff, ed., *Nicene and Post-Nicene Fathers of the Christian Church,* Second Series (Reprint, Grand Rapids: Eerdmans, 1978), 14:264–65. Hereafter abbreviated as *NPNF.*

[26]These two clauses oppose Nestorianism, which divided Christ into two persons, one divine and the other human. As we have seen, depending on which of its mutually exclusive mistaken views of the incarnation it propounds at a given time, Oneness Christology can be a variety of Nestorianism.

[27]These two clauses opposed Eutychianism, which taught that in the incarnation the human and divine natures were mixed, fused, or confounded, the former being absorbed into the latter. See Philip Schaff, *The Creeds of Christendom,* 3 vols. (Grand Rapids: Baker, 1977), 2:65.

[28]This opposed Apollinarianism, which denied the completeness of the human nature in Christ by teaching that the Logos took the place of the human spirit in the incarnation. We have seen that Oneness writers sometimes make this mistake.

[29]This clause opposed Arianism, which had denied the real deity of the Word and was condemned at the Councils of Nicaea in A.D. 325 and Constantinople in A.D. 381 in the Nicene Creed. See E. Calvin Beisner, *God in Three Persons* (Wheaton, Ill.: Tyndale House, 1984), *passim.*

[30]This clause opposed Docetism, which taught that the human body was an illusion, and Apollinarianism, which taught that the Logos took the part of the human spirit in the incarnation, the latter a mistake that Oneness writers sometimes make.

[31]Against the Arians, who denied the deity and eternity of the Son. Oneness writers also deny the eternity of the Son of God, making the title refer only to Christ's human nature.

[32]Reiterating the reality of Christ's humanity, against docetics and Apollinarians, and evading the charge of Nestorians and Arians that if Mary were the mother of God (*Theotokos*) then she herself must be eternal. The reply was that she was the mother of God (the *person* of the Logos) not according to his eternal divine nature but according to his temporal human nature.

[33]Schaff's translation (*Creeds,* 2:62). That the authors of the creed here called him both "Son" and "*monogenē,*" and that the title *Lord* intervenes between the two, indicates that *monogenē* did not mean that

(10) "must be confessed to be in two natures, unconfusedly, immutably,[34]

(11) "indivisibly, inseparably [united],[35]

(12) "and that without the distinction of natures being taken away by such union, but rather the peculiar property of each nature being preserved[36]

(13) "and being united in one Person and subsistence, not separated or divided into two persons,[37] but one and the same Son and only-begotten, God the Word, our Lord Jesus Christ...."

  b. So far as the contrast between Oneness and historic orthodoxy is concerned, the following points summarize the substance of orthodox Christology:

(1) The Word, who at the incarnation was named Jesus, is very God;

(2) The Word is the eternal Son of God, eternally distinct from the Father;

(3) The Word became man;

(4) Although the Word is neither the Father nor the Holy Spirit, "all the fullness of the Deity lives in bodily form" in Christ (Col. 2:9).

(5) Jesus Christ is a single person who, since his incarnation, subsists in two distinct (unconfused, unmixed) natures, deity and humanity, and made atonement for sin as both God and man.

2. The Word, who at the incarnation was named Jesus, is very God (John 1:1; Col. 2:9; Titus 2:13; 2 Peter 1:1).[38] Oneness writers agree.[39]

3. The Word is the eternal Son of God, eternally distinct from the Father.

  a. John 1:1

(1) John 1:1b reveals an eternal, personal distinction in the Godhead involving the Word in personal relationship, or commu-

---

Christ was the only (Son) *begotten* by God the Father. Reflecting the New Testament, the creeds referred to the begetting at the incarnation as done not by the Father but by the Holy Spirit (Luke 1:35). Like the Fathers generally before Jerome (the first to translate *monogenēs*, wrongly, as *unigenitus*, "only-begotten"), the authors of the creed properly understood *monogenēs* to mean "unique, only one of its kind," coming from *monos* (one) and *genos* (kind), not *gennaō* (beget, bear, give birth).

[34]The last four words oppose the Monophysites, who taught that the union of the two natures resulted in a third nature that was neither God nor man.

[35]The last three words oppose Nestorianism's belief in two persons, a divine and a human, in Christ, and the suggestion that the Word might someday abandon the human nature as no longer necessary, both ideas that we have seen in some modern Oneness writers.

[36]These last two clauses oppose Eutychianism and Monophysitism.

[37]Against the Nestorians, and consequently also against modern Oneness Christology.

[38]In Eph. 5:5; 2 Thess. 1:12; 1 Tim. 5:21; 6:13; 2 Tim. 4:1; and 2 Peter 1:2, the Greek grammar indicates that Jesus Christ is called God. See also John 20:28; Rom. 9:5.

[39]Bernard, *Oneness of God*, 61, 188–89; Magee, *Is Jesus*, 40–41; John Paterson, *God in Christ Jesus* (Hazelwood, Mo.: Word Aflame Press, 1966), 9–10, 17; Robert Brent Graves, *The God of Two Testaments* (N.p., 1977), 138–39.

nion, with another person in the Godhead: "In the beginning was the Word, *and the Word was with* [Greek: *prós*] *God*, and the Word was God" (emphasis added).

(a) The Greek phrase "to be with [*prós*] someone" always denotes a relationship between persons.[40] It means to be by, at, near, or in company with someone.[41]

(b) Greek scholar A. T. Robertson observes concerning 2 Corinthians 5:8 ["to be ... at home with the Lord"]: "It is the face-to-face converse with the Lord that Paul has in mind. So John thus conceives the fellowship between the Logos and God" and "In ... (John 1:1) the literal idea comes out well, 'face to face with God.'"[42]

(c) According to New Testament scholar Murray J. Harris, the full import of John 1:1b is, therefore, "'the Word was (in active communion) with the Father.' This seems to be the import of John's statement, whether or not *pros* bears a dynamic sense, for when *pros* describes a relationship between persons it must connote personal intercourse rather than simply spatial juxtaposition or personal accompaniment. Used of divine persons, the prep[osition] points to eternal intercommunion."[43]

(2) That the person John had in mind, with whom the Word was, is the Father, is apparent from the parallel passage in 1 John 1:1–2, where "the Word of life," which is "the life" (see also John 1:4; 14:6), "was with the [*ēn pròs tòn*; same words as in John 1:1b] Father."

b. Colossians 1:13–17

(1) Note carefully the progression of relative pronouns: the Father (v. 12) "brought us into the kingdom of *the Son* he loves, in *whom* [the Son] we have redemption, the forgiveness of sins. *He* [the Son] is the image of the invisible God, the firstborn over all creation. For by *him* [the Son] all things were created ...; all things were created by *him* [the Son] and for *him* [the Son]. *He* [the Son] is before all things, and in *him* [the Son] all things hold together" (emphasis added).

(2) *The Son* created all things, is before all things, and holds all things together.

---

[40] A. T. Robertson, *A Grammar of the Greek New Testament in the Light of Historical Research* (Nashville: Broadman, 1934), 625.

[41] Bauer, *Lexicon*, 711.

[42] Robertson, *Grammar*, 623, 625. So also Nigel Turner, *Syntax*, Vol. 3 of James H. Moulton, *A Grammar of New Testament Greek*, 4 vols. (Edinburgh: T. & T. Clark, 1963), 273–74; George B. Winer, *A Grammar of the Idiom of the New Testament*, 7th ed. (Andover: Warren F. Draper, 1881), 405; and Murray J. Harris, "Prepositions," in *NIDNTT*, 3:1171–1215, esp. 1204–5.

[43] *NIDNTT*, 3:1205.

    (3) Therefore, Paul did not have in mind *solely* the human nature of Christ, but he used the term *Son* to refer to the eternal person and divine nature of Christ.

  c. John 11:27

    (1) This verse calls Jesus "the Son of God, who was *to come into* the world" (emphasis added).

    (2) The English preposition *into* expresses motion toward a goal that requires prior existence in one place and movement into another.

    (3) Similarly, the Greek preposition translated "into" here, *eis*, especially when it follows verbs denoting motion (as here), expresses motion from one place into another.[44]

    (4) Thus the Son of God *was somewhere not* in the world and then *came into* the world.

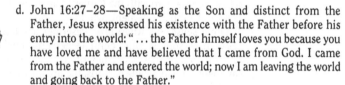

  d. John 16:27–28—Speaking as the Son and distinct from the Father, Jesus expressed his existence with the Father before his entry into the world: " ... the Father himself loves you because you have loved me and have believed that I came from God. I came from the Father and entered the world; now I am leaving the world and going back to the Father."

  e. John 17:1, 4–5

    (1) Jesus, speaking as the Son, claimed to have shared the Father's glory before creation: "Father, the time has come. Glorify your Son, that your Son may glorify you. . . . I have brought you glory *on earth* by completing the work you gave me to do. And now, Father, glorify me in your presence with the glory *I had with you before the world began*" (emphasis added).

    (2) The contrast between *on earth* and *before the world began* signals the antithetical circumstances of the glory the Son brought the Father (on earth) and the glory the Son had in the Father's presence (before the world began).

    (3) The texts make it clear that *the Son* had this glory, that he had it *with*[45] the Father, and that he had it with the Father *before the world was*.

  f. Hebrews 1:1–12—The opening verses of Hebrews attribute both the origin and the sustaining of creation to the Son, call the Son God, and describe the Son as eternally unchanging, as is seen by following the progression of relative pronouns.

---

[44]Bauer, *Lexicon*, 228.

[45]*With* translates the Greek preposition *pará*, which, when followed by the dative case and used of the relationship between persons (as here), indicates being "near, beside." See Bauer, *Lexicon*, 610; see also B. F. Westcott, *The Gospel According to St. John* (1881; reprint, Grand Rapids: Eerdmans, 1991), 240.

g. Galatians 4:4, 6

   (1) The sending forth of the Son to be born of Mary presupposes the Son's prior existence: "But when the time had fully come, God *sent [forth]* his Son, born of a woman.... Because you are sons, God *sent [forth]* the Spirit of his Son into our hearts ..." (emphasis added).

   (2) Bernard objects: "The Son was sent from God as a man, not as God:

     (a) "'God sent forth his Son, made of a woman' (Galatians 4:4).

     (b) "The word *sent* does not imply preexistence of the Son or preexistence of the man. John 1:6 states that John the Baptist was a man sent from God, and we know he did not preexist his conception."[46]

   (3) But:

     (a) God's sending forth of the Son "born of a woman" applies to Jesus' human nature and does not imply that the Son did not exist in his divine nature beforehand.

     (b) The word translated "sent [forth]" in Galatians 4:4, 6 (*exapostéllō*, "to send out, send away," implying prior existence in a location other than that to which one is sent) is not the same as the word translated "sent" in John 1:6 (*apostéllō*, "to send," implying nothing about prior existence), so "sent" in John 1:6 does not explain "sent [forth]" in Galatians 4:4, 6.[47]

4. The Word became man. Consistent with much Old and New Testament usage, the word *flesh* in John 1:14 ("The Word became flesh") denotes not merely the physical body but *the whole man, the human being*.[48]

5. Although the Word is neither the Father nor the Holy Spirit, "all the fullness of the Deity lives in bodily form" in Christ (Col. 2:9).

  a. The Word (Jesus) is not the Father.

   (1) "*I* am the true vine, and *my Father* is the gardener.... As *the Father* has loved *me*, so have I loved you. Now remain in my love. If you obey my commands, you will remain in my love, just as *I* have obeyed *my Father's* commands and remain in his love.... He who hates *me* hates *my Father* as well.... they have hated both *me* and *my Father*" (John 15:1, 9–10, 23–25; emphasis added).

   (2) "I tell you the truth, my Father will give you whatever you ask in my name.... I am not saying that *I* will ask *the Father* on your behalf. No, *the Father* himself loves you because you have loved

---

[46]Bernard, *Oneness of God,* 184.
[47]Bauer, *Lexicon,* 98–99; M&M, *Vocabulary,* 69, 222; Liddell & Scott, *Lexicon,* 212, 586.
[48]Bauer, *Lexicon,* 743; Westcott, *John,* 10–11.

23

me and have believed that I came from God. *I* came from *the Father* and entered the world; now *I* am leaving the world and going back to *the Father*" (John 16:23, 26–28; emphasis added).

(3) "Father, the time has come. Glorify your Son, that *your Son* may glorify *you*.... Now this is eternal life: that they may know *you*, the only true God, *and Jesus Christ*, whom you have sent. *I* have brought *you* glory on earth by completing the work *you* gave *me* to do. And now, Father, glorify me in your presence with the glory *I* had with *you* before the world began.... Righteous Father, though the world does not know *you*, *I* know *you*, and they know that *you* have sent *me*. *I* have made *you* known to them, and will continue to make you known in order that the love *you* have for *me* may be in them and that I myself may be in them" (John 17:1, 3–5, 25–26; emphasis added).

(4) Compare the entire Upper Room Discourse of Jesus in John 14–17.

b. The Word (Jesus) is not the Holy Spirit.

(1) "I will ask the Father, and he will give you another Counselor to be with you forever—the Spirit of truth.... But the Counselor, the Holy Spirit, whom the Father will send in my name, will teach you all things and will remind you of everything I have said to you" (John 14:16, 26).

(2) "When *the Counselor* comes, whom *I* will send to you from the Father, the Spirit of truth who goes out from the Father, *he* will testify about *me*" (John 15:26; emphasis added).

(3) "... Unless *I* go away, *the Counselor* will not come to you; but if I go, *I* will send *him* to you.... But when he, the Spirit of truth, comes, he will guide you into all truth. He will not speak on his own; he will speak only what he hears.... *He* will bring glory to *me* by taking from what is mine and making it known to you" (John 16:7, 13–15; emphasis added).

c. Nonetheless "all the fullness of the Deity lives in bodily form" in Christ (Col. 2:9). This is because the three divine persons possess one and the same divine nature in its entirety.

6. Jesus Christ is one person who, since his incarnation, subsists in two distinct (unconfused, unmixed) natures, deity and humanity, and made atonement for sin as both God and man.

a. Jesus is one person (a single thinking, feeling, and acting agent; see Eph. 4:4–6; 1 Cor. 1:13; 8:6; John 1:14).

b. Since his incarnation, Jesus exists in two distinct natures, without confusion or separation, so that the one person is fully God and fully human.

(1) Jesus is fully God (Titus 2:13; 2 Peter 1:1; 1 John 5:20; John 20:28).

(2) Jesus is fully man (John 1:14; 1 Tim. 2:5; Rom. 5:17, 19).

(3) In the incarnate Jesus, the two natures are not confused into a single new, third nature that is neither God nor man but a mixture of the two; instead, the natures remain distinct while united in one person.

   (a) God is by nature infinite (Eph. 1:23; Jer. 23:23–24; Ps. 139:7–12), eternal (Ps. 90:2; 102:25–27; Isa. 57:15; 44:6), and unchangeable (James 1:17; Num. 23:19; Mal. 3:6).

   (b) Human beings are by nature finite (Ps. 8:3–4), temporal (Ps. 90:9–10), and changeable (Ps. 90:3–6).

   (c) The same nature cannot be simultaneously infinite and finite; eternal and temporal; unchangeable and changeable.

(4) If the person of Christ (the Logos, Jesus, the Son of God, and the Son of Man), who died on the cross, was neither truly God nor truly man but a third thing, a hybrid of the two, then he was not infinite and therefore not capable of paying the full penalty for sin, and he was not human and therefore not properly the representative of sinful human beings, and consequently his death could not atone for man's sin.

(5) But it was as fully God and fully man in one person that Jesus made atonement for sin and became mediator between God and men (Matt. 20:28; Acts 20:28; Heb. 1:3; 2:11, 14–17).

II. Theology: Oneness vs. the Trinity

A. *Basic Statement of the Oneness Position*

   1. In general, Oneness writers teach that there is only one God;

   2. The Father is God;

   3. Jesus is God;

   4. The Holy Spirit is God; and

   5. Jesus = the Father = the Holy Spirit.

B. *Arguments Used by Oneness Writers to Support Their Theology*

   1. Arguments Based on Scripture

      a. There is only one God (see, e.g., Deut. 6:4; 1 Tim. 2:5).[49]

      b. The Father is God (see, e.g., Mal. 2:10; 1 Cor. 8:6).[50]

      c. Jesus is God (see, e.g., John 1:1; 20:28; Titus 2:13).

---

[49]See, e.g., David Bernard, C. A. Brewer, and P. D. Buford, *Meet the United Pentecostal Church International* (Hazelwood, Mo.: Word Aflame Press, 1989), 57–58; J. L. Hall, *The United Pentecostal Church and the Evangelical Movement* (Hazelwood, Mo.: Word Aflame Press, 1990), 28; and Kenneth V. Reeves, *The Godhead,* 7th rev. ed. (Granite City, Ill.: Inspirational Books and Tapes, 1962), 21; Bernard, *Oneness of God,* 13, 16–20; Graves, *God,* 9–10, 57, 71–72, 93.

[50]Bernard, *Oneness of God,* 126.

d. The Holy Spirit is God.

    (1) The terms *God* and *Holy Spirit* are interchangeable. "The Holy Spirit is simply God. God is holy (Leviticus 11:44; I Peter 1:16).... God is also a Spirit (John 4:24), and there is only one Spirit of God (I Corinthians 12:11; Ephesians 4:4). Therefore, 'Holy Spirit' is another term for the one God."[51]

    (2) "That the Holy Ghost is God is evident from a comparison of Acts 5:3 with 5:4 and from a comparison of I Corinthians 3:16 with 6:19. These passages identify the Holy Ghost with God Himself."[52]

e. Jesus = the Father = the Holy Spirit.

    (1) The Bible calls Jesus the Father.

        (a) "Isaiah 9:6 calls the Son the everlasting Father. Jesus is the Son prophesied about and there is only one Father (Malachi 2:10; Ephesians 4:6), so Jesus must be God the Father."[53]

        (b) "If there is only one God and that God is the Father (Malachi 2:10), and if Jesus is God, then it logically follows that Jesus is the Father."[54]

        (c) In John 8:19, 24–25, and 27 "... Jesus Himself taught that He was the Father."[55]

        (d) "In another place Jesus said, 'I and my Father are one' (John 10:30)."[56]

        (e) "Jesus promised to be the Father of all overcomers (Revelation 21:6–7)."[57]

        (f) "For example, Jesus stated in John 12:45, 'And he that seeth me seeth him that sent me.' In other words, if a person sees Jesus as to His deity, he sees the Father."[58]

        (g) In John 14:7–11, Jesus claimed to be the Father. "This statement ... can be viewed as nothing less tha[n] the claim of Christ to be the Father manifested in the flesh."[59]

    (2) The Bible attributes the same works to Jesus and the Father: raising Jesus' body (John 2:19–21; Acts 2:24); sending the Comforter (John 14:26; 16:7); drawing men to God (John 6:44; 12:32); raising believers' bodies (John 6:40; Rom. 4:17; 1 Cor.

---

[51]Ibid., 128.
[52]Ibid.
[53]Ibid., 66.
[54]Ibid.
[55]Ibid., 67.
[56]Ibid.
[57]Ibid., 68.
[58]Ibid., 67–68.
[59]Ibid., 68.

6:14); answering prayer (John 14:14; 16:23); sanctifying (Eph. 5:26; Jude 1).[60]

(3) The Bible calls Jesus the Holy Spirit.

    (a) "There is but one Spirit (Ephesians 4:4). There is but one Lord (I Corinthians 8:6, NIV). 'Now the Lord [Jesus is the one Lord] is the Spirit' (II Corinthians 3:17, NIV)."[61]

    (b) "The Holy Spirit is the Spirit that was incarnated in Jesus and is Jesus in Spirit form (John 14:16–18; Romans 8:9–11; Philippians 1:19; Colossians 1:27)."[62]

(4) The Bible attributes the same things to Jesus and the Holy Spirit, implying that Jesus is the Holy Spirit: "1. Who is the abiding One? Matthew 28:20 says Jesus; John 14:16 says the Spirit. 2. Who makes intercession? Hebrews 4:15 and 7:25 say Jesus; Romans 8:26 says the Spirit. 3. Who is the Paraclete? First John 2:1 says Jesus . . .; John 14:26 says the Spirit. 4. Who is the speaker in Revelation 2–3? Revelation 1:8–12 and 22:16 say Jesus; Revelation 2:7 says the Spirit. Do we have two abiding ones, two intercessors, two Paracletes, and two speakers giving the messages to the seven churches? The answer every time is in the negative."[63]

(5) A technical point of New Testament Greek grammar—the grammatical peculiarities of the conjunction *kai* ("and") and the definite article *ho* ("the")—reveals that the Father, Jesus, and the Holy Spirit are the same person.

    (a) ". . . Granville Sharp's rule means that when two nouns (of the same case) are connected by 'and,' the nouns always refer to *one* person, place, or thing if only the first noun has the Greek definite article before it."[64] E.g.:

        (i) ". . . our great God and Savior, Jesus Christ" (Titus 2:13). Here *God* has the article and *Savior, Jesus Christ* does not, showing that the latter denotes the same person as the former.

        (ii) The same occurs in 2 Peter 1:1: ". . . our God and Savior Jesus Christ."

    (b) Some verses, properly translated according to this rule, show that Jesus and the Father are the same.

        (i) First Corinthians 1:3 should be translated, not ". . . from God our Father, and from the Lord Jesus Christ"

---

[60]Ibid., 69.

[61]Magee, *Is Jesus*, 25 (brackets original).

[62]David K. Bernard, *Oneness and Trinity A.D. 100–300: The Doctrine of God in Ancient Christian Writings* (Hazelwood, Mo.: Word Aflame Press, 1991), 10.

[63]Magee, *Is Jesus*, 26.

[64]Graves, *God*, 143.

(as in KJV), but "... from God our Father and Lord Jesus Christ," or "... from God our Father, *even* the Lord Jesus Christ."[65]

(ii) Colossians 2:2 should be translated, not "... the mystery of God, and of the Father, and of Christ" (as in KJV), but "... the mystery of God—*even* of the Father—*even* of Christ...."[66]

(iii) "... the *KJV* translates *kai* as 'and' in II Corinthians 1:2 but as 'even' in verse 3: Verse 2 says, 'from God our Father, and from the Lord Jesus Christ,' while verse 3 says, 'God, even the Father of our Lord Jesus Christ.' The *KJV* translates *kai* as 'even' in several other places, including the phrases 'God, even the Father' (I Corinthians 15:24; James 3:9) and 'God, even our Father' (I Thessalonians 3:13). So the greetings could read just as easily, 'from God our Father, even the Lord Jesus Christ."[67]

2. Arguments Based on Reason
  a. The doctrine of the Trinity is illogical.
    (1) "... three can never be one *in the same sense* in which they are three, nor can one be three *in the sense* in which it is one. To illustrate: in the example of three sides of a triangle, it is obvious that no single side IS a triangle, would they have us believe that Christ is only one-third of God!"[68]

    (2) "If the Second Person of the Godhead became man in the incarnation, and the Third Person filled Him after He was baptized by John the Baptist, and Jesus said that the Father dwelt in Him (which would be the First Person in Trinitarian theory), then in Jesus Christ dwelt the First, Second and Third Persons of this sublime Trinity. This would be in effect admitting, in a circuitous way, the view they condemn in what they are fond of calling the 'Jesus Only' people."[69]

    (3) "'Would you explain to me, please, how a divine person could pray in His divinity without undeifying Himself?' If we ever hear someone praying, we know they need help, and God most assuredly does not need help."[70]

    (4) "A classic example of the confusion of thought implicit in trinitarian belief is seen when, under questioning, they are obliged

---

[65]Graves, *God*, 50–52.
[66]Graves, *God*, 53–54; Cited similarly by Bernard, *Oneness*, 209.
[67]Bernard, *Oneness*, 208–9.
[68]Paterson, *God*, 69.
[69]Reeves, *Godhead*, 56.
[70]Magee, *Is Jesus*, 18.

to confess that Christ must have had two fathers, namely, the first person of the trinity (they say), to whom He prayed, and the Holy Spirit, who performed the miracle act of paternity in the virgin womb (Luke 1:35)."[71]

(5) "Mark 13:32 and Matthew 24:36 say that the Son does not know the day or hour of His second advent, but only the Father does. According to trinitarianism, there are three omniscient persons in the Godhead. How then does only one divine person (the Father) know the time of the advent?"[72]

(6) Trinitarians defend their belief from logical criticism by saying the Trinity is a mystery. In contrast, "The oneness of God is not a mystery."[73]

b. The terminology of Trinitarianism is unbiblical.

(1) " . . . the terms 'trinity,' 'trinitarian,' 'three persons,' and 'triune God' are not . . . in the Bible. . . . this fact alone ought to cause us to ask . . . where such terminology did come from. . . . In order to combat confusion and heresy, let us strive to *call* Bible things by Bible names. . . ."[74]

(2) "The term 'person' is not accurate terminology to use in reference to the Father or the Holy Ghost" because it "'connotes a human being with a human personality, an individual with a body, soul, and spirit. Thus, we limit our conception of God if we describe Him as a person.'"[75]

(3) " . . . the term 'God the Son' is inappropriate because it equates the Son with deity alone, and therefore it is unscriptural."[76]

3. Arguments Based on History

a. The doctrine of the Trinity is a pagan belief.

(1) Various pagan religions (Assyrian, Babylonian, Egyptian, Hindu, Buddhist, Taoist) and Platonic philosophy believe in some form of divine trinity. "Thus, we can see that the idea of a trinity did not originate with Christendom. It was a significant feature of pagan religions and philosophies. . . ."[77]

(2) "Why did these early theologians make such a blunder [as to believe in the Trinity]? They failed to purge themselves of the pagan ideas of their own past and culture."[78]

---

[71] Ibid., 27.

[72] Ibid., 28.

[73] Bernard, *Oneness and Trinity*, 14.

[74] Graves, *God*, introduction (second unnumbered page). See also Bernard, *Oneness of God*, 262.

[75] Gary C. Rugger, *Oneness, Trinity, Arian: Which One Does Scripture Teach?* (Bakersfield, Calif.: Sarah's Christian Books, 1988), 15, citing Bernard, *Oneness of God*, 287.

[76] Bernard, *Oneness of God*, 99.

[77] Ibid., 264–65.

[78] Ibid., 176.

b. The early church taught Oneness and opposed the Trinity.

(1) " ... none of the second-century [Christian] writers clearly expressed trinitarian orthodoxy, and many of them denied it by such doctrines as the subordination of one divine person to another."[79]

(2) "Clement [of Rome, writing about A.D. 100][80] ... identified the Father as our Creator, Savior, and Lord, which are biblical titles of Jesus."[81]

(3) "The writings of Ignatius (c. 110–15) equate Jesus with the One God so strongly that some historians have called his doctrine modalistic.... Ignatius identified Jesus as the one God manifested in flesh.... Assuming Ignatius understood God to be the Father ... he thought of Jesus as God the Father incarnate."[82]

(4) " ... Ignatius specifically identified Jesus as the indwelling Holy Spirit [in *Magnesians* 15: "The inseparable Spirit, who is Jesus Christ"]."[83]

(5) "Hermas[, in *The Shepherd*, c. 140–45,] did not see the Holy Spirit as a separate person of the Godhead but said He was manifested to the world as the Son: 'The holy, pre-existent Spirit, that created every creature, God made to dwell in flesh, which he chose. This flesh, accordingly, in which the Holy Spirit dwelt, was nobly subject to that Spirit' (Sim. 5:6).... 'I wish to explain to you what the Holy Spirit ... showed you, for that Spirit is the Son of God (Sim. 9:1)."[84]

(6) "Justin's *First Apology* (c. 150) teaches a plurality in the Godhead.... According to [*First Apology* 6 and 13], the Father is the true God. The Son and Spirit are secondary deities similar to angels.... Justin equated the Son with the Word and distinguished the Word as a separate being from the Father. 'For they who affirm that the Son is the Father, are proved neither to have become acquainted with the Father, nor to know that the Father of the universe has a Son; who also, being the first-begotten Word of God, is even God' ([*First Apology*], 63)."[85]

---

[79]Ibid., 24.

[80]Bernard leans toward late dates for Clement and other early Christian writers discussed below. A growing body of scholarship supports much earlier dates. On this, see John A. T. Robinson, *Redating the New Testament* (Philadelphia: Westminster, 1976), 352–53. Robinson dates 1 Clement no later than A.D. 70 and perhaps as early as A.D. 68.

[81]Bernard, *Oneness and Trinity*, 30.

[82]Ibid., 33.

[83]Ibid., 33–34.

[84]Ibid., 39–41.

[85]Ibid., 65–66.

(7) "Although Justin identified the Holy Spirit as a third being to worship, he did not distinguish the Spirit clearly from the Father and the Word or define the relationship among these three. Indeed, in several places he identified the Spirit as the Word. For example, [he writes in] his *First Apology* ... [that] 'it is wrong ... to understand the Spirit and the power of God as anything else than the Word, who is also the first-born of God' (33). ..."[86]

(8) "Since [Justin's disciple] Tatian held that the Logos was originally inherent in the Father, his *Diatessaron* [a harmony of the gospels] rendered the last phrase of John 1:1 as, 'God is the Word.' In effect, he interpreted John 1:1 much as Oneness believers do today. As far as eternity past is concerned he apparently had a Oneness concept. He differed from Oneness in teaching that at a certain point in time before the creation of the world the Word came out of God as a distinct person."[87]

C. Refutation of Arguments for Oneness and Against the Trinity

1. Scripture refutes Oneness arguments against the Trinity. Historic, biblical Christianity

    a. Agrees that there is only one God,

    b. Agrees that the Father is God,

    c. Agrees that Jesus is God,

    d. Agrees that the Holy Spirit is God. However,

        (1) The terms *God* and *Holy Spirit* are not interchangeable.

        (a) Bernard commits the fallacy of equivocation by assuming that every use of *spirit* (capitalized or not) in reference to God must denote the Holy Spirit. But in John 4:24, *pneûma* ("spirit") lacks the definite article and is a predicate nominative preceding the (implied) verb "to be," making it qualitative, telling what sort of thing God is (spirit, not matter). Thus it is not a personal designation.[88]

        (b) His argument based on 1 Corinthians 12:11 and Ephesians 4:4 fails to prove that only one spirit is holy. In both verses, the term *Holy Spirit* is used as a proper name, not as a common noun preceded by an adjective. Further, in neither verse does the word *holy* occur in the Greek; it is inferred in translation, so the verses cannot properly be used in Bernard's argument. In neither case does the fact

---

[86]Ibid., 68–69.

[87]Ibid., 79–80.

[88]For this principle of Greek grammar, see H. E. Dana and Julius R. Mantey, *A Manual Grammar of the Greek New Testament* (New York: Macmillan, 1955), 150; and Philip B. Harner, "Qualitative Anarthrous Predicate Nouns: Mark 15:39 and John 1:1," *Journal of Biblical Literature* 92 (1973): 75–87.

that there is but one Holy Spirit (proper name) mean no other spirits are holy (e.g., angels). That God is spirit and is holy, therefore, does not equate God and the Holy Spirit.

(2) Acts 5:3–4, 1 Corinthians 3:16, and 6:19 do support the deity of the Holy Spirit.

e. Finally, biblical Christianity *denies* that Jesus = the Father = the Holy Spirit.

(1) The Bible does not call Jesus the Father.

(a) Simply finding Jesus (the Son) called "father" (Isa. 9:6; Mal. 2:10; Eph. 4:6) does not prove He is God the Father, since *father* is a relational term, its sense determined by the relationship in mind. (I am a father, but I am not *my* father.) Oneness writers must prove Jesus is called specifically the Father of the Son of God (i.e., his own Father). Isaiah 9:6 only calls him "father of eternity."

(b) The argument that if (1) there is only one God, and (2) that God is the Father (Mal. 2:10), and (3) Jesus is God, then Jesus is the Father, begs the question (assumes something contested) by assuming that God is *only* the Father.

(c) Jesus did not teach "that He was the Father" in John 8:19, 24–25, 27.

(i) By leaving out John 8:26, Bernard makes it look as if John's explanation ("He was telling them about his Father," v. 27) applied to Jesus' answer to the Pharisees' question in verse 25, that is, as if John meant Jesus had claimed to be "his Father."

(ii) But in verse 26 Jesus said, "I have much to say in judgment of you. But *he who sent me* is reliable, and what I have heard from *him* I tell the world" (emphasis added).

(iii) John's explanation in verse 27 then is clear: *the One who sent him* and from whom he had heard was his Father.

(iv) The passage distinguishes Jesus and the Father.

(v) Furthermore, according to Oneness Christology, since Jesus here speaks of "my Father," he must be speaking as the Son. But if so, and if Bernard's interpretation is correct, then it is as the Son that he claims to be the Father. But this contradicts the Oneness insistence that the Son is not the Father but is only the human nature of the incarnate Jesus.

(d) Jesus does not claim to be the Father in John 10:30.

(i) Jesus did not say, "I am the [or "my"] Father," he said, "I and the Father are one."

    (ii) Jesus used the plural form of the verb *to be* ("are"), indicating that the two subjects are distinct persons.

    (iii) Jesus used the neuter word for *one* (Gk. *hen*), not the masculine, thus claiming unity not of person but of essence or nature.[89]

    (iv) Again, if the Oneness interpretation is correct, then since Jesus speaks here as the Son (v. 36), the Son is the Father, which Oneness denies.

    (v) The actual sense of Jesus' claim is that he and the Father are the same God (not the same person), precisely what Trinitarianism says and what the Jews understood him to claim (10:33).

(e) Revelation 21:6–7 does not mean that Jesus is God the Father.

    (i) It is not Jesus but "He who was seated on the throne" (21:5) who says of him who overcomes, "I will be his God and he will be my son." "He who was seated on the throne" is the Father (Rev. 3:21; 4:2–3, 9–11; 5:1, 6–7, 13; 6:16; 7:10, 14–15; 19:4; 20:11) and is distinguished from the Lamb (5:13; 6:16; 7:10), who (1) has his own throne (3:21), though Christ's throne and the Father's throne are closely associated, and (2) "came and took the scroll from the right hand of him who sat on the throne" (5:7).

    (ii) Even if Jesus were speaking in these verses, that would not prove that he is the Father, since he only says, "he who overcomes . . . will be my son" (21:7), that is, that he will be a father to overcomers, not to himself.

(f) John 12:45 does not prove that Jesus is the Father.

    (i) In the context, Jesus distinguishes himself from the one who sent him: "When a man believes in me, he does not believe in me only, but in the one who sent me" (12:44) and "When he looks at *me*, he sees *the one who sent* me" (12:45, emphasis added; see also 49–50).

    (ii) The distinction cannot be explained by the Oneness hermeneutic that distinguishes between the human and divine natures of Jesus, for then the "me" in verse 45 at whom people "look" would have to be divine and

---

[89]A. T. Robertson, *Word Pictures in the New Testament,* 6 vols. (Nashville: Broadman, 1932), 5:186. See also Westcott, *John,* 159; R. C. H. Lenski, *The Interpretation of St. John's Gospel* (Minneapolis: Augsburg, 1961), 759–60.

thus invisible (since the divine nature is spirit [John 4:24] and cannot be seen by men [John 1:18]).

(g) Jesus did not claim to be the Father in John 14:7–11.

(i) Jesus distinguishes himself from the Father by using prepositions to show a relationship between them: "No one comes *to* the Father except *through* me" (14:6); "I am *in* the Father, and ... the Father is *in* me" (14:10–11); the Father is "living *in* me" (14:10); "I am going *to* the Father" (14:12, all emphases added).

(ii) He explicitly contrasts himself with the Father when he says, "The words I say to you are not just my own. Rather, it is the Father, living in me, who is doing his work" (14:10).

(iii) Jesus consistently uses first person pronouns of himself ("I" and "me") and a third person pronoun of his Father ("him"), thus showing the distinction between them.

(iv) Oneness arguments focus on the words, "Anyone who has seen me has seen the Father" (14:9). But the only thing people could *see* of Jesus was his body, which Oneness Christology (like Trinitarian theology) denies was divine. Thus he cannot have spoken literally when he said that whoever *saw* him *saw* the Father, so he must have spoken figuratively.

(2) Attributing the same things to Jesus and the Father does not prove that Jesus is the Father. Arguing so is an example of hasty generalization.

(a) Since the Bible does not say that *only* the Father or *only* Jesus can do or be these things, it does not follow logically that Jesus must be the Father.

(b) Since only God can do these things, attributing them to Jesus does prove that Jesus is God, but not that he is the Father, which is the point in debate.

(3) The Bible does not call Jesus the Holy Spirit.

(a) Comparing Ephesians 4:4, 1 Corinthians 8:6, and 2 Corinthians 3:17 does not show that Jesus is the Holy Spirit, since doing so equivocates on the meanings of *spirit* and *lord* in the verses.

(i) There are many spirits other than the Holy Spirit, both literal (e.g., angels, demons, the spirits of men, and the spirit that is God's substance [John 4:24]) and metaphorical (e.g., the spirit of holiness [Rom. 1:4], of the law [Rom. 7:6] or covenant [2 Cor. 3:6, 8], etc.), with some holy (e.g., angels), and others not (e.g., demons).

(ii) The word *Spirit* in Ephesians 4:4 denotes the Holy Spirit (note the contrast between "one Spirit" and "one Lord" and "one God and Father of us all," 4:4–6), while the word *spirit* in 2 Corinthians 3:17 may instead denote the essence of God.[90]

(iii) The word *Lord* in 1 Corinthians 8:6 denotes Jesus,[91] while in 2 Corinthians 3:17 it may instead denote Jehovah.[92]

(iv) To assume that *spirit* in both Ephesians 4:4 and 2 Corinthians 3:17 denotes the Holy Spirit and *Lord* in both 1 Corinthians 8:6 and 2 Corinthians 3:17 denotes Jesus is to argue in a circle by assuming what Oneness must prove.

(b) The Bible does not say that the Holy Spirit was incarnated and is Jesus in spirit form.

(i) In John 14:16–18, Jesus expressly distinguishes himself from the Holy Spirit by calling him "another Counselor" than himself and by using third person pronouns to denote the "Counselor," but first person pronouns to denote himself. Likewise, his saying that the disciples know the Spirit "for he lives with you and will be in you" and that he himself "will come to you" asserts an intensely intimate unity between himself and the Spirit, but not an identity with each other.

(ii) Romans 8:9–11, Philippians 1:19, and Colossians 1:27 do not say that Christ is the Spirit.

(4) Since the Bible does not say that *only* Jesus or *only* the Spirit can do or be these things, it does not follow logically that Jesus must be the Spirit just because the Bible attributes the same things to Jesus and the Spirit, any more than that dogs are cats just because dogs are mammals and cats are mammals.

---

[90]Albert Barnes, *Barnes' Notes on the New Testament,* ed. Ingram Cobbin (Grand Rapids: Kregel, 1976), 830–31; Robert Jamieson, A. R. Fausset, and David Brown, *A Commentary, Critical, Experimental, and Practical on the Old and New Testaments,* 3 vols. (Reprint, Grand Rapids: Eerdmans, 1976), 3:2:345; John Calvin, *Commentary on the Epistles of Paul the Apostle to the Corinthians,* trans. John Pringle, vol. 20 of *Calvin's Commentaries* (Reprint, Grand Rapids: Baker, 1984), 2:164–88.

[91]1 Cor. 8:6 teaches only that one Lord is in special relationship to believers, not that there is only one lord at all. Also, the word *kúrios* ("lord") in the New Testament refers some 667 times to Jesus or God and 82 times to some nondivine lord, master, sir, or owner. See J. B. Smith, *Greek-English Concordance to the New Testament* (Scottdale, Pa.: Herald Press, 1955), 210.

[92]Compare Ex. 34:29–35, and see Robertson, *Word Pictures,* 4:223; E. Cadman Colwell, "A Definite Rule for the Use of the Article in the Greek New Testament," *Journal of Biblical Literature* 52 (1933): 18.

(5) The grammatical peculiarities of the Greek conjunction *kai* ("and") and the Greek definite article *ho* ("the") do not reveal that the Father, Jesus Christ, and the Holy Spirit are the same person. Whether to translate *kai* as "and" or "even" is not an arbitrary choice but is governed by rules of grammar.

    (a) Apparently thinking it to be a single rule, Graves cites only the first of six rules discovered by Granville Sharp.

        (i) The first three describe grammatical constructions in which the nouns connected by *kai* denote *the same* thing or person. Graves rightly cites Titus 2:13 and 2 Peter 1:1 as examples.

        (ii) But the last three describe constructions in which the nouns connected by *kai* denote *distinct* things or persons.

    (b) None of the verses cited by Graves and Bernard (or any others not cited by them), translated according to the relevant rules, calls Jesus the Father. Also, Graves and Bernard mistranslate the verses that they do cite.

        (i) First Corinthians 1:3 exemplifies not Sharp's rule #1 but #5, which means the nouns denote distinct persons. Therefore, Graves's translations are wrong.

        (ii) According to Sharp's rule #6, the repetition of the article *toû* (the) between *kaì* (and) and *Christoû* (Christ) in Colossians 2:2 shows that *Christoû* names a different person from that named by *theoû kaì patròs* (God and Father).

        (iii) Thinking it is analogous to 2 Corinthians 1:3, Bernard wrongly translates 2 Corinthians 1:2 as "from God our Father, even the Lord Jesus Christ." But the relevant clauses are not analogous.[93] According to Sharp's rule #5, "God our Father" should be distinguished from "the Lord Jesus Christ."

2. The doctrine of the Trinity is not contrary to reason.

    a. Oneness logical arguments against the doctrine of the Trinity all commit logical fallacies.

        (1) The doctrine of the Trinity does not hold that three are one *in the same sense* in which they are three, but that Father, Son,

---

[93]Specifically, the Greek in 2 Cor. 1:2 is *theoû patròs hēmōn kaì kuríou Iēsoû Christoû*; none of the nouns is preceded by the article and all are in the genitive case. On the other hand, the Greek in 1:3 is *ho theòs kaì patēr toû kuríou hēmōn Iēsoû Christoû*; the words *theòs* and *kuríou* both are preceded by the article, and *theòs* is in the nominative case while *kuríou* is in the genitive case. Therefore, 1:2 is not properly translated "from God our Father, even the Lord Jesus Christ" but, according to Sharp's rule #5, "from God our Father and [from] the Lord Jesus Christ," showing the personal distinction between "God our Father" and "the Lord Jesus Christ."

and Spirit are one in the sense that they are the same God but three in the sense that they are distinct persons. Thus Paterson attacks a straw man.

(2) Acknowledging that the Father and the Holy Spirit indwelt the incarnate Son does not contradict the Trinitarian distinction of persons, for "being X" and "indwelling X" are not synonymous.

(3) That Jesus prayed does not disprove the Trinity.

(a) Magee's argument, if valid, would disprove Jesus' deity, which Oneness affirms. If Jesus' prayers are consistent with his being God, then they are also consistent with his being distinct from the Father.

(b) Praying for help is not inconsistent with Jesus' being God as well as man, for as man he *did* need help.

(c) Jesus' prayers are inconsistent with the Oneness view of God and the incarnation, for according to Oneness theology, Jesus could pray to no other person since Jesus himself was the Father and the Holy Spirit.

(d) The Oneness reply that the human nature of Jesus prayed to the divine nature fails because it implies that Jesus is two persons; persons pray, not natures.

(4) Magee's argument that Trinitarianism implies that the Son of God had two Fathers fails because

(a) the Father's paternity and the Word's sonship did not originate at the conception in Mary's womb but are eternal, and

(b) the Spirit conceived not the divine but the human nature of Jesus in the womb of Mary.

(5) Mark 13:32 and Matthew 24:36 do not imply that either the Son or the Holy Spirit lacks omniscience.

(a) If they did, they would equally disprove the Oneness doctrine of Christ.

(i) Knowing is an act of the mind.

(ii) The incarnate Christ had but one mind (1 Cor. 2:16; Phil. 2:5).

(iii) Therefore, whatever the incarnate Christ knew, he knew with his one mind, which was divine even while he was united personally to the human nature, including human intellect.

(iv) Thus, if Christ was actually ignorant of the time of his coming, he was ignorant of it as God, which is impossible (1 John 3:20).

37

       (v) Therefore, to be consistent with their own Christology, Oneness writers should interpret these verses so as not to imply that the Son did not know when he would return.

    (b) The verses are best interpreted not as literally denying the Son's knowledge of when he would return (compare Gen. 18:20–21; 22:12; compare Ps. 147:5; 1 John 3:20;[94] John 21:17; see also Col. 2:3; Matt. 9:4; Mark 5:30; 9:33; John 11:34) but as his declining to divulge the knowledge to the disciples.

  (6) Far from making it preferable to Trinitarianism, the claim that the "oneness of God is not a mystery" implies that Oneness is false.

    (a) First Timothy 3:16 calls the incarnation of God in Christ a mystery.

    (b) Therefore, any theology with no mysterious elements is sub- or antibiblical.

    (c) Bernard's objection to calling a doctrine mysterious is special pleading, since he himself calls Oneness Christology a mystery.[95]

    (d) In the Bible, *mystery* denotes not something illogical or irrational but something secret or hidden (Deut. 29:29; Rom. 11:25; 1 Cor. 15:51), especially if later revealed (Col. 1:26–27; 2:2; 4:3).[96] By calling the Trinity a mystery, Trinitarians mean that some aspects of God are beyond human discovery without revelation, not irrational.

    (e) Christ's incarnation involved precisely such a revealing of what was once hidden (John 1:18).

 b. Oneness arguments do not prove that the use of extrabiblical terminology in Trinitarianism is illegitimate.

  (1) What is important is not whether *terminology* is found in Scripture but whether, in substance, the terminology expresses *truths* of Scripture.

  (2) That the Bible does not use *Trinity* (or any other term) is no more evidence against Trinitarianism than the absence of the word *Oneness* in the Bible is evidence against Oneness theology. When Oneness writers argue this way, they indulge in special pleading.

---

[94]See E. Calvin Beisner, "The Omniscience of God: Biblical Doctrine and Answers to Objections," *Crosswinds* 2, no. 1 (Spring/Summer 1993): 10–26.

[95]Bernard, *Oneness of God,* 64.

[96]Bauer, *Lexicon*, 530–31.

3. Oneness historical arguments do not disprove the doctrine of the Trinity.

   a. They do not prove that the doctrine of the Trinity is a pagan belief.

      (1) The fact that various pagan religions believe in some form of trinity does not prove that the doctrine of the Trinity is pagan.

          (a) Many pagan religions believe in a creator; that does not mean that biblical Christianity, which also believes in a creator, is pagan.

          (b) The various "trinities" of pagan religions actually are not analogous to the Christian Trinity but are tritheistic (Assyrian, Babylonian, Egyptian, Hindu, and others) or emanational and impersonal (Platonic philosophy).[97]

      (2) Bernard's accusation that Trinitarian theologians "failed to purge themselves of the pagan ideas of their own past and culture"

          (a) begs the question, assuming that the doctrine of the Trinity was borrowed from pagan religions or philosophy, while that is in debate; and

          (b) fails to recognize that the modalist view of God better resembles certain pagan religious beliefs (like the Hindu notion of God as Brahman [the absolute and undivided One] revealed in three modes as Brahma [creator], Vishnu [preserver], and Shiva [destroyer]) and Platonic philosophy than does the doctrine of the Trinity.

   b. Oneness historical arguments do not prove that the early church believed in Oneness.[98]

      (1) If, as Bernard alleges, many second-century Christian writers implicitly denied the Trinity[99] by asserting "the subordination of one divine person to another," much more so did they implicitly deny Oneness.

          (a) Although it affirms their equality of nature, Trinitarianism acknowledges a subordination of will by the Son to the Father and of the Spirit to the Father and the Son, and therefore can incorporate the sort of subordination affirmed by the early Church Fathers.

---

[97]Benjamin B. Warfield, "Trinity," in *The International Standard Bible Encyclopedia,* ed. James Orr et al., 5 vols. (1956, reprint; Peabody, Mass.: Hendrickson, 1994), 3012.

[98]Bernard and other Oneness writers cite more patristic passages than are discussed here, but analysis similar to the following shows that they fail to establish their point. Space prohibits discussing all their citations here, but I hope to do so in a larger book.

[99]There is an implicit inconsistency in Bernard's argument here. Elsewhere he argues from the word *trinity*'s not being used in the Bible or by early Christian writers to the conclusion that the doctrine of the Trinity is not biblical and was not taught by the early Christian writers. But if early Christian writers could implicitly *deny* the doctrine, they must also have been capable of implicitly *affirming* it; and similarly also Scripture.

(b) Oneness, however, denies any distinction of persons in God and therefore can admit no subordination.

(2) Since Clement does not say that *only* the Father or *only* Jesus is Creator, Savior, or Lord, his attributing titles to the Father that the Bible attributes to Jesus is not evidence against the Trinity; thus Bernard's argument is hasty generalization.

(3) Ignatius's calling Jesus God manifest in the flesh does not equate Jesus with the Father or teach modalism.

(a) Trinitarians also call Jesus God incarnate but do not equate Father and Son.

(b) Bernard's inference is fallacious. It assumes that (i) if Jesus is God and (ii) if God is the Father, then (iii) Jesus must be the Father. But premise (ii), taken to mean that God is *only the Father*, as it must be for Bernard's conclusion to follow, is debated between Oneness and Trinitarianism. To assume it is to beg the question.

(4) Ignatius did not call Jesus the Holy Spirit.

(a) Bernard arbitrarily assumes that *spirit* in *Magnesians* 15 denotes the Holy Spirit.

(b) But *spirit* can denote other things, and the sense of *attitude*, *mind*, or *demeanor* better suits the context.[100]

(5) Hermas's understanding of the Holy Spirit is unclear, but it does not necessarily support Oneness or contradict the Trinity. For example, although Hermas writes of the "holy, pre-existent Spirit" as having been made to dwell in flesh, he later writes of the flesh in which this "holy, pre-existent Spirit" already dwelt as having been chosen by God "as a partner with the Holy Spirit," implying a distinction between the "holy, pre-existent Spirit" that dwelt in the flesh of Jesus and the "Holy Spirit" with whom he was a partner (*Similitude* 5:6).

(6) Justin's teaching, whether consistent with orthodox Trinitarianism or not, certainly contradicts Oneness.

(a) Bernard admits: "Justin's *First Apology* (c. 150) teaches a plurality in the Godhead."

(b) Bernard wrongly asserts that Justin "distinguished the Word as a separate *being* from the Father" (emphasis added). While Justin denied that "the Son is the Father," he also asserted that the Son, "being the first-begotten Word of God, is even God." And since he insisted that there

---

[100]J. B. Lightfoot and J. R. Harmer, trans., *The Apostolic Fathers: Revised Greek Texts with Introductions and English Translations* (Reprint, Grand Rapids: Baker, 1984), 146; J. B. Lightfoot, ed. and trans., *The Apostolic Fathers: Clement, Ignatius, and Polycarp, Revised Texts with Introductions, Notes, Dissertations, and Translations*, 5 vols. (Reprint, Peabody, Mass.: Hendrickson, 1989), 2:2:140.

is only one God (*Dialogue with Trypho,* 11), he cannot have meant that the Son was a separate *being* (separate God) from the Father.

(7) Bernard wrongly asserts that Justin "identified the Holy Spirit as a third *being* to worship" (emphasis added) and "identified the Spirit as the Word."

  (a) Nowhere can he cite Justin calling the spirit "a third *being*" from the Father and the Son, and if all Justin meant by writing of "the true God" in the first place, "the Son" in the second, and "the prophetic Spirit in the third" was that the Spirit was a third *person* (though the same being), then his view was consistent with the Trinity; either way, it contradicted Oneness.

  (b) Justin's insistence that "we ought to worship God alone" (*First Apology,* 16) and that "to God alone we render worship" (17), coupled with his belief that the Holy Spirit is to be worshiped (6) implies that the Spirit is *not* a third being but the same God as the Father and the Son, who, together with the Spirit, are to be worshiped (6).

  (c) Justin's enumerating "the prophetic Spirit" as "in the third" place to the Father and the Son in our worship (*First Apology,* 13) proves that he distinguished the Spirit from Jesus Christ.

  (d) Therefore, interpreting "the Spirit [or "spirit"] and power of God" as denoting the Holy Spirit, as Bernard does, means making Justin contradict himself when he adds that it is wrong "to understand the [s]pirit and power of God as anything else than the Word" (*First Apology,* 33).

  (e) It is more likely, therefore, that Justin had in mind not the Holy Spirit but simply the substance (John 4:24, "God is spirit") and power of God.

(8) Tatian's doctrine of the Logos did fall short of a Trinitarian conception,

  (a) but it contradicted Oneness theology, since Tatian believed that the Logos was distinct from the Father even before creation.[101]

  (b) Bernard's inference depends on assuming that *God* is subject and *Word* is predicate nominative, but here *God* is

---

[101]See his *Pros Helleōnas* (*Oration to the Greeks*), 5, in J.-P. Migné, ed., *Patrologiæ Græcæ,* 6:813–15). Compare the J. E. Ryland translation in Alexander Roberts and James Donaldson, eds., *The Ante-Nicene Fathers: Translations of the Writings of the Fathers down to* A.D. *325,* 10 vols. (Reprint, Grand Rapids: Eerdmans, 1975), 2:67 (hereafter referred to as *ANF*), with the translation and discussion in Bethune-Baker, *History,* 126–27.

predicate nominative and *Word* is subject, just as in John 1:1c in Greek, which Tatian here copied.[102]

D. Arguments Used to Prove the Doctrine of the Trinity to a Oneness Adherent

1. Basic Statement of the Doctrine of the Trinity

    a. Orthodox Christianity confesses, as in the *Athanasian Creed*,[103]

        (1) " . . . we worship one God in Trinity, and Trinity in Unity;[104]

           (a) "neither confounding the persons,

           (b) "nor dividing the substance [essence].[105]

        (2) "For there is one Person of the Father, another of the Son, and another of the Holy Ghost.

        (3) "But the Godhead of the Father, of the Son, and of the Holy Ghost, is all one:[106]

           (a) "the glory equal, the majesty coeternal.

           (b) "Such as the Father is, such is the Son, and such is the Holy Ghost;

           (c) "the Father uncreated, the Son uncreated, and the Holy Ghost uncreated;

           (d) "the Father unlimited, the Son unlimited, and the Holy Ghost unlimited;

           (e) "the Father eternal, the Son eternal, and the Holy Ghost eternal.

        (4) "And yet they are not three eternals, but one eternal.

           (a) "As also there are not three uncreated, nor three infinites, but one uncreated, and one infinite.

---

[102]See D. Plooij, *A Primitive Text of the Diatessaron: The Liège Manuscript of a Mediæval Dutch Translation, A Preliminary Study* (Leyden: A. W. Sijthoff's Uitgeversmaatschappij, 1923), introductory note by J. Rendel Harris, 3.

[103]It is called this not because it is by Athanasius but because it expresses most precisely the Trinitarian doctrine defended by Athanasius and officially adopted in the Nicene Creed (Schaff, *Creeds*, 1:36). First adopted at Nicea in A.D. 325 and slightly revised and confirmed at Constantinople in A.D. 381, the Nicene Creed was the first creedal statement endorsed by church leaders (bishops, elders, and deacons) from throughout the Mediterranean and Middle East, the region in which Christianity had spread the most. It clearly and officially stated the doctrine of the Trinity. The doctrine had been implied in earlier creeds of more or less official weight and stated more or less explicitly in apologetic writings dating back at least to the middle of the second century (*Creeds*, 2:40–41). The Nicene Creed is affirmed in most of the major creeds of Eastern and Western churches, including Catholic, Orthodox, and Protestant (*Creeds*, 2:207, 279, 456; 3:7, 95, 362, 393, 492, 528). The Athanasian Creed is affirmed in many of the same creeds.

[104]Oneness apologists beg the question when they insist that they alone believe in the unity of God. Trinitarianism affirms both the unity and the trinity of God.

[105]Affirming the *unity* of the divine essence against those who would conceive of the persons as three gods.

[106]Affirming the unity of the divine essence and, as developed in the following points, the equal participation of all three persons in that one undivided essence, against an essential (as opposed to economic) subordinationism. These points ([3] and [4] and their subpoints) affirm that all of the attributes of deity are shared equally by all three persons.

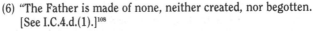
(b) "So likewise the Father is almighty, the Son almighty, and the Holy Ghost almighty. And yet they are not three almighties, but one Almighty.

(c) "So the Father is God, the Son is God, and the Holy Ghost is God. And yet they are not three Gods, but one God.

(d) "So likewise the Father is Lord, the Son is Lord, and the Holy Ghost is Lord. And yet not three Lords, but one Lord.

(5) "For like as we are compelled by the Christian verity to acknowledge every person by himself to be God and Lord, so are we forbidden by the catholic[107] religion to say, 'There are three Gods, or three Lords.'

(6) "The Father is made of none, neither created, nor begotten. [See I.C.4.d.(1).][108]

(7) "The Son is of the Father alone, not made, nor created, but begotten.

(8) "The Holy Ghost is of the Father and of the Son, neither made, nor created, nor begotten, but proceeding.

(9) "So there is one Father, not three Fathers; one Son, not three Sons; one Holy Ghost, not three Holy Ghosts.

(10) "And in this Trinity none is before or after another. But the whole three persons are coeternal and coequal, so that in all things, as aforesaid, the Unity in Trinity, and the Trinity in Unity, is to be worshipped."[109]

b. Summary

(1) There is only one God.

(2) The Father is God.

(3) The Son is God.

(4) The Spirit is God.

(5) The Father and the Son are distinct persons.

(6) The Father and the Spirit are distinct persons.

(7) The Son and the Spirit are distinct persons.

2. Arguments Based on Scripture

a. There is only one God (Deut. 4:34; 6:4; Isa. 43:10–11; Matt. 28:19; 1 Cor. 8:4–6; 1 Tim. 2:5). Agreed.

b. The Father is God (Matt. 28:19; John 17:3; Rom. 1:7; 1 Cor. 1:3). Agreed.

---

[107]The word *catholic* is used here in the sense of "universal"—i.e., this is the view held everywhere and by all true Christians—not in the later sense of "Roman Catholic."

[108]Points (6), (7), and (8) name the incommunicable attributes of the persons, i.e., those that are not shared by more than one of the persons. The Father's incommunicable attribute is that he begets the Son; the Son's, that he is begotten by the Father; and the Spirit's, that he proceeds from the Father and the Son.

[109]Adapted (with outline numbers and modernized punctuation) from Schaff, *Creeds*, 2:66–68.

c. Jesus (the Word, the Son of God) is God (Matt. 28:19; John 1:1; 20:28; Rom. 9:5; Titus 2:13). Agreed. However, modern Oneness theology denies that he is God *as the Son of God,* insisting that he is Son only in his human nature. Against this, see I.C.4 and I.D.3.

d. The Holy Spirit is God (Gen. 1:2; Matt. 28:19; 2 Cor. 13:14; see also Acts 5:3–4). Agreed.

e. The Father and the Son are distinct persons.

(1) The Father and the Son glorify each other both before and after the incarnation (John 17:1, 4–5).

(2) They are distinct as judge and judged in the atoning sacrifice of Christ (Mark 15:34; Luke 23:46).

(3) They were distinct at creation: " ... the Father ... brought us into the kingdom of the Son he loves, ... by him [the Son] all things were created" (Col. 1:12–13, 16).

(4) "It is my Father who gives you the true bread from heaven. For the bread of God is he who comes down from heaven. ... I am the bread. ... I have come down from heaven not to do my will but to do the will of him who sent me" (John 6:32–33, 35, 38).

(a) The Father sends the "bread" (Jesus).

(b) The bread "comes down from heaven."

(c) The "bread" therefore existed in heaven prior to coming down from heaven.

(d) The very Jesus who "came down from heaven" and therefore existed in heaven prior to coming down from heaven came "not to do [his own] will but to do the will of [the Father] who sent [him]."

(5) The Father and Jesus are distinguished as two witnesses (John 8:14–18).

(a) Jesus cannot be speaking here merely as human, for he claims to have come from heaven (8:14; see also 6:62; 8:54–58; 13:3; 16:26–28).

(b) Therefore the distinction between the two witnesses is between the Father as divine and Jesus (the Son) as divine.

(c) If Jesus and the Father were the same person, there would be only one person testifying of Jesus, and therefore his testimony would be invalid (John 5:31), but Jesus expressly said, "There is another who testifies in my favor, and I know that his testimony about me is valid" (John 5:32), and this other is the Father (v. 37).

(6) Jesus and the Father were distinct in heaven before the incarnation (John 8:38; 20:17).

(a) This cannot be merely his human nature speaking, for that did not come from the Father's presence (see also 6:62; 8:14–18; 13:3; 16:26–28).

(b) Yet the distinction between him and his Father is as real as that between the disciples and their Father (however different it may be).

(7) The Father and the Son, as God, are referred to as "both the Father and the Son" (2 John 9), showing their distinction as divine persons.

(8) In 2 John 3, the repetition of *from* (*parà*) emphasizes the distinction between Father and Son.

f. The Father and the Holy Spirit are distinct persons.

(1) The Holy Spirit is a person, not simply the substance (spirit, John 4:24) of God.

(a) John 4:24 does not mean that God is *the Holy Spirit*, for the predicate nominative, *spirit*, is not preceded by the article and therefore is neither definite ("the Spirit") nor indefinite ("a spirit") but qualitative ("God is spirit").[110]

(b) The Gospel of John applies personal language to the Holy Spirit just as to Father and Son.

(i) Although the world does not "know" him, the disciples "know" him, that is, in personal relationship (John 14:17).

(ii) In John 16:13–14, John emphasizes the Spirit's personality by using a masculine emphatic pronoun (*ekeînos*) to denote him, despite the Greek word for "spirit" (*pneûma*) being neuter.[111]

(2) The Father will "give the Holy Spirit to those who ask him" (Luke 11:13; see also John 14:16; Eph. 1:17).

(3) The Father sends the Holy Spirit (John 14:25–26), showing a distinction between the sender and the one sent.

g. Jesus and the Holy Spirit are distinct persons.

(1) Jesus drives out demons *not* by himself *but* "by the Spirit of God ..." (Matt. 12:28).

(2) Blasphemy against the Son of Man (a title that encompasses his divine nature, since the Son of man "came from heaven" [John 3:13]; "has authority on earth to forgive sins," which "God alone" can do [Mark 2:10, 7]; and "is Lord of the Sabbath" [Matt. 12:8]) can be forgiven, but not blasphemy against the Holy Spirit (Matt. 12:31–33).

---

[110]Westcott, *John*, 73; Lenski, *John*, 324–25; Robertson, *Word Pictures*, 5:67.

[111]Many interpreters add John 14:26 and 15:26 to the list (e.g., Edmund J. Fortman, *The Triune God: A Historical Study of the Doctrine of the Trinity* [Grand Rapids: Baker, 1982], 28; Westcott, *John*, 209). However, in those verses the masculine *ekeînos* may not correlate with the neuter *pneûma* but with the masculine *parákleōtos* (Comforter). In 16:13–14, however, *ekeînos* clearly correlates with *pneûma*. See Robertson, *Word Pictures*, 5:255, 263, 268; Robertson, *Grammar*, 709; Lenski, *John*, 1090; Westcott, *John*, 231.

(3) The Holy Spirit testifies about Jesus as Jesus' Paraclete with believers (John 15:26).

(4) Jesus sends the Holy Spirit as someone distinct from himself (John 15:26; 16:7–11).

h. Specific passages denote Father, Son, and Spirit as distinct from each other: "And *I* [the Son] will ask the Father, and *he* will give you *another Counselor* [the Holy Spirit] to be with you forever" (John 14:16; see also 14:26; 15:26; 16:15).

i. According to Sharp's rules of grammar, the grammatical peculiarities of the conjunction *kai* ("and") and the definite article *ho*[112] ("the") reveal that the Father, the Son, and the Holy Spirit are distinct persons.[113]

(1) Sharp's first three rules define constructions in which two or more personal nouns linked by *kai* must denote the same person. No instance of these constructions in the New Testament implies that Father, Son, and Holy Spirit are the same person. However, some instances reveal that

(a) the Father is God (Gal. 1:4, rule #1; Eph. 1:17, rule #2; Col. 1:2, rule #3), and

(b) the Son is God (Eph. 5:5, rule #1); Titus 1:3; 2 Peter 2:1, rule #3).

(2) Sharp's fourth rule exempts *impersonal* nouns from rules 1–3 and 5–6.

(3) Sharp's fifth and sixth rules define constructions in which two or more personal nouns linked by *kai* must denote *distinct persons.* Several such instances reveal that the Father, the Son, and the Holy Spirit are distinct persons.

(a) *When the first noun lacks the article,* each noun must denote a *distinct person* (rule #5)—e.g., Rom. 1:7 and Gal. 1:1, Christ is distinct from the Father.[114]

(b) *When each noun is preceded by the article,* each noun must denote a *distinct person* (rule #6)—e.g., Matt. 28:19,

---

[112]And its various declensions (forms) by number, gender, and case.

[113]The grammatical issues are highly technical and can receive only cursory treatment here. But since some Oneness writers have cited these rules as though they support their position (e.g., Bernard, *Oneness of God,* 208–11; Graves, *God,* 50–55, 133–35, 143–45), it is necessary to observe that they have misunderstood Sharp's six rules. (In fact, they write as if there were only one rule instead of six.) Indeed, these rules not only fail to support the Oneness position but refute it. Those who know Greek can confirm the accuracy of the conclusions drawn here by consulting C. Kuehne, "The Greek Article and the Doctrine of Christ's Deity," *Journal of Theology: Church of the Lutheran Confession* 13, no. 3 (September 1973): 12–28; 13, no. 4 (December 1973): 14–30; 14, no. 1 (March 1974): 8–19; 15, no. 1 (March 1975): 8–22, in which Kuehne brilliantly explains, illustrates, and defends the six parts of Sharp's rule.

[114]On Rom. 1:7, see the identical construction in 1 Cor. 1:3; 2 Cor. 1:2; Gal. 1:3; Eph. 1:2; 6:23; Phil. 1:2; 1 Thess. 1:1; 2 Thess. 1:1–2; Philem. 1:3. On Gal. 1:1, see similarly 1 Tim. 1:1–2; 2 Tim. 1:2; Titus 1:4; Philem. 1:3.

"the Father and ... the Son and ... the Holy Spirit" are distinct persons;[115] 1 Thess. 3:11, "our God and Father ... and our Lord Jesus" are distinct persons; 2 Thess. 2:16–17, "our Lord Jesus Christ ... and God our Father" are distinct persons;[116] 1 John 2:22–23, "the Father and the Son" are distinct persons; Rev. 5:13, "him who sits on the throne and ... the Lamb" are distinct persons; Rev. 11:15, "our Lord and ... his Christ" are distinct persons.

3. Arguments from Reason

   a. Trinitarianism is logically consistent.

      (1) Substance and person are distinct categories of things.

      (2) Therefore, a single substance (being) may be no person (e.g., a rock), one person (e.g., a human being), or more than one person (God), just as a single person (Christ) may be more than one substance (Deity and humanity).

      (3) The doctrine of the Trinity states that one undivided substance (Deity) is three persons.

   b. The use of extrabiblical terminology is legitimate.

      (1) *Trinity:* Properly understood, the term adds nothing to what Scripture reveals regarding God. "When we have said these three things, then,

         (a) "that there is but one God,

         (b) "that the Father and the Son and the Spirit is each God,

         (c) "that the Father and the Son and the Spirit is each a distinct person, we have enunciated the doctrine of the Trinity in its completeness."[117]

      (2) Person(s):

         (a) The term *person* can properly denote self-conscious things other than human beings, such as angels, demons, imaginary self-conscious beings, and each of the three persons of God.

---

[115]Oneness writers sometimes claim that the one name mentioned in Matthew 28:19 is "Jesus" (see Bernard, *Oneness of God,* 136–40). But their argument begs the question by presupposing that the name Jesus elsewhere applies to the Father and the Holy Spirit, a claim refuted above. One name that does apply to Father, Son, and Holy Spirit, and that would have been prominent in the minds of Jesus' Jewish disciples, is Jehovah; to call the Father, the Son, and the Holy Spirit each Jehovah while maintaining their personal distinction by repeating the article before each personal noun is to affirm the Trinity.

[116]Oneness writers sometimes point to 1 Thessalonians 3:11 and 2 Thessalonians 2:16–17 as proofs that Father and Son name just one person because of the singular verbs (Graves, *God,* 58–59). However, in each instance the subject of the verb is not "our God and Father ... and our Lord Jesus" (1 Thess. 3:11) or "our Lord Jesus Christ ... and God our Father" (2 Thess. 2:16–17), but the singular emphatic pronoun *Autós,* "He," which is why the verb must be singular. In both instances, applying Sharp's rule #6 shows that "our God and Father" is distinct from "our Lord Jesus" and that "our Lord Jesus Christ" is distinct from "God our Father." What we are told, then, in each instance is that the Father and Jesus, though distinct persons, are still the one God.

[117]Warfield, "Trinity," 3016.

(b) Properly understood, the term, applied to the Father, the Son, and the Spirit, adds nothing to what Scripture reveals about God. "The Scriptural facts are,

  (i) " ... The Father says I; the Son says I; the Spirit says I.

  (ii) " ... The Father says Thou to the Son, and the Son says Thou to the Father; and in like manner the Father and the Son use the pronouns He and Him in reference to the Spirit [and to each other].

  (iii) " ... The Father loves the Son; the Son loves the Father; the Spirit testifies of the Son. The Father, Son, and Spirit are severally subject and object. They act [upon each other] and are acted upon [by each other]. . . .

  (iv) "Nothing is added to these facts when it is said that the Father, Son, and Spirit are distinct persons; for a person is an intelligent subject who can say I, who can be addressed as Thou, and who can act and be the object of action.

  (v) "The summation of the above facts is expressed in the proposition, The one divine Being subsists in three persons, Father, Son, and Spirit. This proposition adds nothing to the facts themselves; for the facts are, . . . That there is [only] one divine Being ... Father, Son, and Spirit are divine ... Father, Son, and Spirit are, in the sense just stated, distinct persons."[118]

4. Arguments Based on Tradition:

The doctrine of the Trinity is implied in the writings of the early church fathers.[119]

  a. They taught that there is but one God.[120] Oneness and Trinitarianism agree.

  b. They taught that the Father is God.[121] Oneness and Trinitarianism agree.

---

[118]Charles Hodge, *Systematic Theology*, 3 vols. (Grand Rapids: Eerdmans, 1973), 1:444.

[119]In what follows, we shall focus on the most important writings of the period of the apostolic fathers, the latter half of the first and the early second centuries. The doctrine of the Trinity is much more pronounced in later writers, but modern Oneness writers admit that. They claim, however, that these earlier writings taught modalism (see Bernard, *Oneness and Trinity*, 42–45; William B. Chalfant, *Ancient Champions of Oneness: A History of the True Church of Jesus Christ* [Junction City, Kans., 1979]).

[120]E.g., Clement of Rome, *Corinthians*, 59; *Magnesians*, 8; Hermas, *The Shepherd*, Mandate 1, in Lightfoot and Harmer, *The Apostolic Fathers*, 82, 144, 422.

[121]Clement of Rome, *Corinthians*, 62; Ignatius, *Ephesians*, inscription; Polycarp, *Philippians*, 12; in Lightfoot and Harmer, *Apostolic Fathers*, 84 (English) and 39 (Greek), 137 (English) and 105 (Greek), 181 (English) and 173 (Latin).

   c. They taught that Jesus (the Son) is God.[122] Oneness and Trinitarianism agree.

   d. They taught that the Holy Spirit is God.[123] Oneness and Trinitarianism agree.

   e. Contradicting Oneness but supporting Trinitarianism, they taught that the Father and the Son (not merely the human nature of Jesus but the divine Son of God both before and after his incarnation) are distinct persons.

     (1) Ignatius distinguishes the Father from the Son.[124] He writes:

        (a) of "the bountifulness of the Father Most High and of Jesus Christ His only Son" (*Romans,* inscription),

        (b) of the Apostles' being "obedient to Christ and to the Father" (*Magnesians,* 13:2; see also *Magnesians,* inscription; 1:2; 13:1;[125] *Ephesians,* 21:2; *Trallians* 1:1;[126] *Philadelphians,* inscription; 1:1; 3:2; *Polycarp,* inscription; and *Smyrnæans,* inscription).[127]

        (c) "of Jesus Christ, who was with the Father before the worlds and appeared at the end of time," who "did nothing without the Father," "who came forth from One Father and is with One and departed unto One," through whom God "manifested Himself," and who "is His [i.e., God's] Word that proceeded from silence, who in all things was well-pleasing unto Him that sent Him" (*Magnesians,* 6–8).[128]

---

[122]In Lightfoot and Harmer, *Apostolic Fathers,* see Clement of Rome, *Corinthians,* 16 (English, p. 63, and Greek, p. 12); Ignatius, *Ephesians,* inscription (English, 137, and Greek, 105), 1:1 (English, 137, and Greek, 105), 7:2 (English, 139, and Greek, 107), 18:2 (English, 141, and Greek, 110), *Romans,* inscription (English, 149, and Greek, 119), 3:3 (English, 150, and Greek, 120), 6:3 (English, 151, and Greek, 122), 7:3 (English, 152, and Greek, 122), *Polycarp,* 3:2 (English, 160, and Greek, 132), 8:2 (English, 162, and Greek, 134), *Smyrnæans,* 1:1 (English, 156, and Greek, 127); Polycarp, *Philippians,* 12.2, probable original Greek (English, 181, and Latin, 173; see Lightfoot, *Apostolic Fathers,* 2:3:476 [English], 346 [Greek and Latin], and 345, where Lightfoot explains why the bracketed words *Son of* before *God Jesus Christ* almost certainly are not original).

[123]In Lightfoot and Harmer, *Apostolic Fathers,* see: Clement, *Corinthians,* 58 (English, p. 82, and Greek, p. 36; see also in Lightfoot, *Apostolic Fathers,* 1:2:301–2 [English] and 169 [Greek]); Ignatius, *Magnesians,* 13:1 (English, 146, and Greek, 115); *Martyrdom of Polycarp,* 14:3 (English, 208, and Greek, 194; see also Lightfoot, *Apostolic Fathers,* 2:3:483 [English], and 388 [Greek]).

[124]When one consults the original Greek text of Ignatius, the Granville Sharp rules referred to above make it clear that he distinguishes the Father from the Son. Never does he use a construction fitting Sharp's rule #1 or rule #2, which would equate Father and Son.

[125]Lightfoot's English translation has *the* before *Son* but not before *Father* and has it again before *Spirit.* But the Greek lacks the article in all three positions. With all due respect for the master Lightfoot, more attentive translating would have treated all three similarly.

[126]The grammar shows that he considered *God* and *Jesus Christ* distinct persons. Yet Ignatius also taught the deity of Christ. The implication is that Ignatius sometimes used the term *God* by itself as a title specifically for God the Father, as often occurs in the New Testament.

[127]See the Greek texts in Lightfoot and Harmer, *Apostolic Fathers.*

[128]Lightfoot and Harmer, *Apostolic Fathers,* 144–45 (English), 113–14 (Greek).

(2) Polycarp: "Now may the God and Father of our Lord Jesus Christ, and the eternal High-priest Himself the God Jesus Christ, build you up in faith and truth ..." (*Philippians* 12:2).[129]

(3) Barnabas: "... the Lord endured to suffer for our souls, though He was Lord of the whole world, unto whom God said from the foundation of the world, Let us make man after our image and likeness.... He manifested Himself to be the Son of God" (*Epistle of Barnabas*, 5:5, 9).[130]

f. They taught that the Son and the Spirit are distinct persons.

(1) Clement: "... our Lord Jesus Christ, came not in the pomp of arrogance or of pride, though He might have done so, but in lowliness of mind, according as the Holy Spirit spake concerning Him" (*Corinthians*, 16:2).[131]

(2) Ignatius: "... our God, Jesus the Christ, was conceived in the womb by Mary according to a dispensation, of the seed of David but also of the Holy Ghost ..." (*Ephesians*, 18:2).[132]

(3) Polycarp wrote that the Father should receive glory *with* Christ *and* the Holy Spirit (*Martyrdom of Polycarp*, 14).[133]

g. They taught that the Father and the Spirit are distinct persons.

(1) Polycarp implied the distinction of the Spirit from the Father when he said that the Father should receive glory *with* Christ and the Spirit (*Martyrdom of Polycarp*, 14).[134]

(2) Hermas implied the distinction of the Spirit from God [the Father] when he wrote, "Put away therefore from thyself sadness, and afflict not the Holy Spirit that dwelleth in thee, lest haply He intercede with God [against thee], and depart from thee" (*The Shepherd*, 10:2:5–6).[135]

h. They referred to all three together as distinct persons.

(1) Clement: "... God liveth, and the Lord Jesus Christ liveth, and the Holy Spirit, who are the faith and the hope of the elect ..." (*Corinthians*, 58).[136]

(2) Polycarp: "O Lord God Almighty, the Father of Thy beloved and blessed Son Jesus Christ, ... I praise Thee, I bless Thee, I glorify Thee, through the eternal and heavenly High-priest Jesus

---

[129]Ibid., 181. The words *Son of* are given in brackets before *God Jesus Christ* in the source, but they are not in the original Greek. See Lightfoot, *Apostolic Fathers*, 2:3:345. See also *Martyrdom of Polycarp*, 14, in Lightfoot, *Apostolic Fathers*, 2:3:483 (English), 387 (Greek).

[130]Lightfoot and Harmer, *Apostolic Fathers*, 273 (English), 247–48 (Greek).

[131]Ibid., 63 (English), 13 (Greek).

[132]Ibid., 141 (English), 110 (Greek).

[133]Lightfoot, *Apostolic Fathers*, 2:3:483 (English), 388 (Greek).

[134]Ibid., 2:3:483 (English), 388 (Greek).

[135]Lightfoot and Harmer, *Apostolic Fathers*, 433 (English), 333 (Greek).

[136]Ibid., 82 (English), 36 (Greek). The repetition of the article (in Greek) before *God* and *Lord Jesus Christ* and *Holy Spirit* (Sharp's rule #6), and the plural verb ("are") both indicate their distinction.

Christ, Thy beloved Son, through whom with Him and the Holy Spirit be glory to Thee both now and for the ages to come. Amen" (*Martyrdom of Polycarp*, 14).[137]

(a) That the Father is to receive glory "through" Christ distinguishes him from Christ.

(b) That Christ and the Holy Spirit are to receive glory "with" the Father indicates that they, like him, are God, and that they are distinct from him.

III. Soteriology (The Doctrine of Salvation): Salvation By Grace Alone or By Grace Plus Works?

A. *Basic Statement of the Oneness Position*

1. In general, Oneness writers teach that in Adam all humankind fell into sin, guilt, and spiritual death; therefore, no one can satisfy God's requirements of perfect righteousness or atone for his or her own sin.

2. Justification is by God's grace through faith in Christ, who died as a substitutionary sacrifice to satisfy the penalty for the sins of all men.

3. Salvation requires a new birth.

4. New birth is achieved by faith, repentance, water baptism, and baptism in the Holy Spirit.

   a. Faith is not mere intellectual assent but moral commitment and trust that bears fruit in a changed life.

   b. Repentance is a turn from sin to righteousness.

   c. Water baptism is the indispensable means of regeneration.

   d. Water baptism is the indispensable means of remission of sin.

   e. Water baptism must be by immersion to be effective.

   f. Water baptism must be administered with a Jesus' name formula to be effective.

   g. Baptism in the Holy Spirit is essential to salvation and never occurs without the "initial evidence" of speaking in tongues.

B. *Arguments in Support of Oneness Soteriology*

1. In Adam, all humankind fell into sin, guilt, and spiritual death; therefore, no one can satisfy God's requirement of perfect righteousness or atone for his or her own sin (Rom. 5:12–19; 1 Cor. 15:21–22, 47–48; Eph. 2:1–5).

---

[137]Lightfoot, *Apostolic Fathers*, 2:3:483 (English), 388 (Greek). The key clause is *di' hoû soi sùn autoō kaì pneúmati hagíō [hē] dóxa kaì nûn [kaì aeì] kaì eis toùs méllontas aiōnas*, literally translated (following the Greek word order), "through whom to you with him and with the Holy Spirit [be] glory both now [and ever] and for the coming ages." In the Greek, the distinction of *soi* (you, second person pronoun) from *autō* (him, third person pronoun) and from *pneúmati hagíō* (Holy Spirit, proper name) is clear.

2. Justification (being "declared righteous and free from guilt and punishment" and receiving the imputation of the righteousness of Christ) is by God's grace through faith in Jesus Christ (John 3:16; Rom. 3:21–31; 6:23; Gal. 2:16–21; Eph. 2:1–10), who died as a substitutionary sacrifice to satisfy the penalty for human sin (Matt. 20:28; Gal. 2:20; 1 Tim. 2:5–6; 1 Peter 2:21, 24; 1 John 2:2).[138]

3. Salvation requires a new birth (John 3:3, 5, 7; 2 Cor. 5:17; Eph. 2:1–5).

4. New birth is achieved by faith, repentance, water baptism, and baptism in the Holy Spirit.

   a. Faith is not mere intellectual assent but moral commitment and trust that bears fruit in a changed life (Rom. 6; James 2:14–26).

   b. Repentance is a turn from sin to righteousness (Jer. 31:19; Matt. 3:7–12; Acts 3:19; 2 Cor. 7:8–11; 2 Tim. 2:24–26; Heb. 6:1; Rev. 2:5).

   c. Water baptism is the indispensable means of regeneration.

      (1) According to John 3:5, "Water baptism is a part of that process by which a man is born into, or made a part of, the kingdom of God. (See Romans 14:17; Col. 1:13–14; [Mark] 16:16.) It is not by water alone, or by Spirit alone, but both elements are needed to effect the new birth."[139]

      (2) According to Titus 3:5, we are saved "through the washing of rebirth and renewal of the Holy Spirit."

      (3) "Baptism is not only a birth, it is a burial. 'We are buried with him by baptism into death . . .' (Romans 6:4). In I Corinthians 15:1–4, Paul explained that the gospel is the death, the burial, and the resurrection of Jesus Christ. In repentance, we identify ourselves with the death of Christ, and His cross. When we are baptized, we identify ourselves with His burial (Colossians 2:12)."[140]

   d. Water baptism is the indispensable means of remission of sin.

      (1) "Baptism is where sins are officially remitted through the name of Jesus Christ (Acts 10:43)."[141]

      (2) "Paul had acknowledged Christ on the Damascus road and had spent three days in fasting and prayer when Ananias told him to 'Arise, and be baptized, and wash away thy sins, calling on the name of the Lord' (Acts 22:16). Those who have repented and believed upon Christ can be cleansed from their sins by the

[138]See Charles Clanton, Dennis Croucher, and Paul Dugas, *Salvation: Key to Eternal Life* (Hazelwood, Mo.: Word Aflame Press, 1985), 106–17.

[139]Charles Clanton, Crawford Coon, and Paul Dugas, *Bible Doctrines: Foundation of the Church* (Hazelwood, Mo.: Word Aflame Press, 1984), 79; see also *Salvation*, 72–73.

[140]Clanton et al., *Bible Doctrines*, 79.

[141]Ibid., 81.

blood of Christ by being baptized in the name of Jesus Christ (I Corinthians 6:11)."[142]

(3) "We should notice the purpose of baptism as stated in Acts 2:38.

    (a) "Water baptism is 'for the remission of sins.' We are to be baptized in the name of Jesus Christ for the purpose of obtaining the remission of sins.

    (b) "The word *for* is translated from the Greek word *eis* and means 'in order to obtain.'"[143]

(4) "Although United Pentecostals recognize that water baptism is 'for the remission of sins' (Acts 2:38), they believe that baptism is effective only by faith in Jesus Christ and by calling upon His name, for there is no salvation without faith and the name of Jesus Christ (Hebrews 11:6; Acts 2:21; 4:12; 10:43; 22:16)."[144]

e. Water baptism must be by immersion to be effective.

(1) "The word *baptize* comes from the Greek words *bapto* and *baptizo*, which mean to plunge, dip, or immerse.... Thus, to baptize anyone correctly, we must immerse him into water."[145]

(2) Romans 6:3–5 and Colossians 2:12 say we are buried with Christ by baptism into death. Therefore, "Any other mode of baptism is incomplete and contrary to the teaching of the Bible."[146]

(3) The early church always baptized by immersion.

f. Water baptism must be administered with a Jesus' name formula ("in the name of the Lord Jesus Christ," or "in the name of Jesus Christ" or "in the name of the Lord Jesus" or "in the name of Jesus" or "in Jesus' name") to be effective.

(1) "Since water baptism is 'for the remission of sins' and since the name of Jesus is the only name that saves from sin (Acts 4:12), it is needful for the name of Jesus to be spoken in water baptism. (See Matthew 1:21; Luke 24:47.)"[147]

(2) " ... baptism identifies the person with Christ (Romans 6:3–4).... baptism is the act of putting on Christ (Galatians 3:27)...."[148]

---

[142]Ibid.

[143]Carl E. Williams, *The Bible Plan of Salvation* (Hazelwood, Mo.: Word Aflame Press, 1988), 11.

[144]Hall, *UPC and Evangelical*, 33.

[145]D. L. Welch, *Contending for the Faith* (Hazelwood, Mo.: Word Aflame Press, 1988), 29. A common claim in Oneness (and other immersionist) discussions of baptism; see also, e.g., Ralph V. Reynolds, *Truth Shall Triumph: A Study of Pentecostal Doctrines* (Hazelwood, Mo.: Word Aflame Press, 1965), 42; Clanton et al., *Bible Doctrines*, 82.

[146]Welch, *Contending*, 29; see also Reynolds, *Truth*, 42.

[147]David Bernard, C. A. Brewer, and P. D. Buford, *Meet the United Pentecostal Church International* (Hazelwood, Mo.: Word Aflame Press, 1989), 50–51.

[148]Ibid.

(3) " ... the early church administered water baptism in the name of Jesus Christ (Acts 2:38; 8:16; 10:48; 19:5; 22:16; Romans 6:3–4; Galatians 3:27; Colossians 2:11–12)."[149]

(4) Historical evidence shows that the Jesus' name formula, not the triune formula, was originally used by the early church, and that the triune formula replaced it only as the church abandoned true monotheism (Oneness or modalism) and embraced pagan Trinitarianism.[150]

"Many encyclopedias and church historians agree that the original baptismal formula in early church history was 'in the name of Jesus.' For example, Lutheran professor Otto Heick says, 'At first baptism was administered in the name of Jesus, but gradually in the name of the Triune God: Father, Son, and Holy Spirit.'"[151]

g. Baptism in the Holy Spirit is essential to salvation and never occurs without the "initial evidence" of speaking in unknown tongues.

(1) "The baptism with, by, in, or of the Holy Ghost (Holy Spirit) is part of New Testament salvation, not an optional, postconversional experience (John 3:5; Romans 8:1–16; Ephesians 1:13–14; Titus 3:5)."[152]

(2) "Anyone who has never spoken in tongues has never been baptized with the Holy Ghost."[153]

(3) "The Bible records five historical accounts of receiving the Holy Spirit in the New Testament church: the Jews, the Samaritans, the Gentiles, the Apostle Paul, and the disciples of John at Ephesus. This record establishes that

(a) The baptism of the Spirit is indeed for everyone (Luke 11:13; Acts 2:39)

(b) And is accompanied by the sign of tongues (Mark 16:17)....

(c) "Three of the accounts explicitly describe speaking in tongues as the initial evidence of receiving the Spirit [Acts 2:1–4; 10:44–48; 19:1–7].... Tongues are implicit in the other two accounts [Acts 8:8, 12–19; 9:17, compare 1 Corinthians 14:18]...."[154]

(4) "How did Peter and the other Jewish brethren know without doubt that these Gentiles had received the Holy Ghost? The

---

[149]Ibid., 51.

[150]See Bernard, *Oneness and Trinity*, ch. 8; and Thomas Weisser, *Jesus' Name Baptism Through the Centuries* (N.p., 1989), *passim*.

[151]Bernard, *Oneness of God*, 138.

[152]David K. Bernard, *Essentials of the New Birth* (Hazelwood, Mo.: Word Aflame Press, 1987), 19.

[153]Reynolds, *Truth*, 53–54. See also Kenneth V. Reeves, *The Holy Ghost with Tongues*, 2d ed. (Granite City, Ill.: Inspirational Tapes and Books, 1991), 8–9.

[154]Bernard, *Essentials*, 19–20.

answer is found in [Acts 10:46]: *For they heard them speak with tongues, and magnify God.* From this account we see clearly that the Early Church recognized speaking in tongues as the initial evidence of receiving the Holy Ghost."[155]

C. Refutation of Arguments for Oneness Soteriology

1. In Adam, all humankind fell into sin, guilt, and spiritual death; therefore, no one can satisfy God's requirements of perfect righteousness or atone for his or her own sin. Agreed.

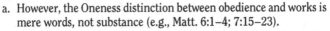

2. Justification (being declared righteous and exempt from guilt and punishment, and receiving the righteousness of Christ) is by God's grace through faith in Jesus Christ, who died as a substitutionary sacrifice to satisfy the penalty for human sin. Agreed.

   a. However, the Oneness distinction between obedience and works is mere words, not substance (e.g., Matt. 6:1–4; 7:15–23).

   b. It is "not because of righteous things [whether we call them obedience or works] we had done, but because of his mercy" that God has saved us (Titus 3:5).

   c. Rather than obedience being a *qualification or condition* of salvation, it is the inevitable *fruit* of real faith, which itself is a gift of God (Eph. 2:8–10).

   d. Therefore, while obedience confirms faith (Matt. 7:15–23), it does not contribute to justification (Rom. 3:19–31; Gal. 2:15–16).

3. Salvation requires a new birth. Agreed.

4. New birth is *not* achieved by faith, repentance, water baptism, and baptism in the Holy Spirit.

   a. Faith is not mere intellectual assent but moral commitment and trust that bears fruit in a changed life. Agreed.

   b. Repentance is a change of mind that necessrily bears fruit in a turn from sin to righteousness. Agreed.

   c. Water baptism is *not* the indispensable means of regeneration.

      (1) For John 3:5 to support baptismal regeneration, the view that *born of water* denotes water baptism must be the only plausible interpretation, but

         (a) *Born of water* could be a figurative allusion to natural birth in response to Nicodemus's statement, "Surely [a man] cannot enter a second time *into his mother's womb* to be born!" (John 3:4, emphasis added). Jesus' response would mean, " . . . no one can enter the kingdom of God unless he is born [not only] of water [(i.e., naturally, from his mother's womb) but also of] the Spirit" (see also 3:6).

---

[155]Oliver F. Fauss, *Baptism in God's Plan* (Hazelwood, Mo.: Word Aflame Press, 1990), 20–21.

55

(b) *Born of water* could be a figurative allusion to being born of the Holy Spirit (see Isa. 12:3; 35:6; 44:3; 55:1; Jer. 2:13; Ezek. 36:25; Zech. 14:8; John 4:10; 7:37–38; Rev. 21:6; see also Ezek. 47:1–5; Rev. 22:17). Then Jesus' response would mean, "No one can enter the kingdom of God unless he is born of water, in other words,[156] of the Spirit," the latter phrase clarifying the former.

   (i) This interpretation gains support from the need to ensure consistency between John 3:5 and 8.

   (ii) If *born of water* denotes neither the natural birth nor being *born of the Spirit* but water baptism, then verse 5 requires both baptism and being born of the Spirit for entry into the kingdom, while verse 8 requires only being born of the Spirit.

   (iii) But if *born of water* denotes being *born of the Spirit*, then verses 5 and 8 require the same thing.

(2) Oneness advocates cite Titus 3:5 to support baptismal regeneration, claiming that *washing of rebirth* denotes water baptism. However,

(a) *Washing of rebirth* may allude to spiritual rebirth (see verses on water as a symbol of the Holy Spirit immediately above), in which case the verse would bear the sense, " ... he saved us, not because of righteous things we had done, but because of his mercy, through the washing of rebirth, in other words,[157] the renewal by the Holy Spirit."

(b) This interpretation relieves the tension between the latter part of the verse and the former created by the view that *washing of rebirth* means water baptism, for

   (i) Water baptism, commanded by God, is a righteous thing we do,

   (ii) But God "saved us, not because of righteous things we had done, but because of his mercy."

   (iii) So if *washing of rebirth* is water baptism, then God saved us "not because of righteous things we had done ... but through baptism [i.e., a righteous thing we do]," which is inconsistent.

(3) Romans 6:4 does not state that baptism is the indispensable means by which we are buried with Christ, only that through it we are so buried; it does not follow that we cannot be so buried apart from it.

---

[156]*Kai*, the Greek word translated *and* in John 3:5, often bears this explicative sense, i.e., connecting one word or clause with another in which the latter explains the former. See Bauer, *Lexicon*, 393; Hodge, *Systematic Theology*, 3:596.

[157]See preceding note.

(4) Not only do these passages not prove that water baptism is indispensable to regeneration, but also Scripture teaches that regeneration sometimes happens before water baptism (Acts 2:41; 8:12; 9:18; 10:47–48; 16:14–15, 30–33; 18:8). But cause must precede effect.

d. Water baptism is *not* the indispensable means of remission of sin.

(1) Acts 10:43 does not mention baptism, much less say it is "where sins are officially remitted." Instead, it says, " . . . everyone who believes in him receives forgiveness of sins through his name."

(2) Acts 22:16 does not prove that water baptism is indispensable to washing away sins.

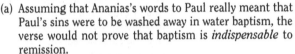

(a) Assuming that Ananias's words to Paul really meant that Paul's sins were to be washed away in water baptism, the verse would not prove that baptism is *indispensable* to remission.

(i) If it were a cause of remission, water baptism could be sufficient but not necessary; necessary and sufficient; necessary but insufficient; or neither necessary nor sufficient but elective.

It cannot be a *sufficient* cause of remission or regeneration, whether necessary or not, because it is ineffective apart from faith (Mark 16:16; Heb. 11:6).

It cannot be a *necessary but insufficient* cause of remission or regeneration, because remission can occur before it (Acts 2:41; 8:12; 9:18; 10:47–48; 16:14–15, 30–33; 18:8; Luke 23:39–43; Rom. 4:9–12; see also Col. 2:11–14).

Therefore, water baptism, even if it were a cause of remission or regeneration, would have to be neither necessary nor sufficient but *elective*; God, the agent of regeneration and remission, may elect to use it or not.

(ii) Scripture sometimes refers to a symbol as if it were the thing symbolized, yet, like bread in communion (John 6:51, 56; Luke 22:19; 1 Cor. 10:16), symbol and thing are not confused; Christ's death, not broken bread, saves. Similarly, water baptism symbolizes our purification from sin (Acts 22:16) and union with Christ in his death, burial, and resurrection (Rom. 6:1–7),[158] yet Christ's blood, not water, washes away

---

[158]Although baptism as a purificatory rite symbolizes purification from sin, it is a sign not only of washing but also of union or identification with Christ and all that this union involves: death, burial, resurrection, and ultimate glorification. See John Murray, *Christian Baptism* (Phillipsburg, N.J.: Presbyterian and Reformed, 1980), 3–5.

sins (Heb. 9:13–14, 22; 1 John 1:7; Rev. 1:5; 7:14; see also 1 Peter 3:21).

We were purified from sin in union with Christ, not with water (Col. 2:11).

Believers legally died to the law (Rom. 7:4) in union with him on the cross, not in water baptism.

We were buried (Rom. 6:4) with him in his burial, not in water baptism.

We rose again from the dead and were seated in heavenly places (Eph. 2:4–6) in union with him in his resurrection, not in water baptism.

(iii) Therefore, neither water nor water baptism but the blood of Christ and its application to us (our union with Christ), *symbolized* by water and its application in baptism, are the real cause of our regeneration and the remission of our sins.

The real purpose of water baptism is not to *cause* regeneration and remission of sins but to *signify* them to assure the faithful recipient that he has them. Like circumcision (Rom. 4:11), water baptism is a *sign*, not the cause, of regeneration and remission of sins.

(3) Acts 2:38 does not teach that baptism is indispensable to remission of sins,

(a) Grammatically, the command to be baptized is not connected with the promise of remission of sins.

(i) The Greek verb translated *repent* is second person plural and in the active voice.

(ii) The Greek verb translated *be baptized* is third person singular and in the passive voice.

(iii) The Greek pronoun translated *your* (in "remission of your sins") is second person plural.

(iv) Therefore, the grammatical connection is between *repent* and *for the remission of your sins*, not between *be baptized* and *for the remission of your sins*.[159]

(b) The phrase *for the remission of your sins* need not mean "in order to obtain the remission of your sins."

(i) *For* translates *eis*, a preposition with many meanings.[160]

---

[159]When I showed this explanation of the verse to the late Dr. Julius R. Mantey, one of the foremost Greek grammarians of the twentieth century and coauthor of Dana and Mantey's *Grammar*, he heartily approved of it and signed his name to the page of my Greek New Testament on which I had written the explanation.

[160]Bauer, *Lexicon*, 228–30.

(ii) One meaning is "to denote reference to a person or thing *for, to, with respect* or *reference to*"[161] (e.g., Matt. 5:13; Luke 14:35; Acts 17:21; Rom. 8:28; 2 Cor. 13:3; Col. 1:12; 2 Tim. 2:21; 4:11; 2 Peter 1:17).

(iii) If this is the meaning of *eis* in Acts 2:38, then even if water baptism is connected with remission of sins, the sense is not that baptism is *in order to obtain* but rather *with reference to* (i.e., as a sign of, or because of) the remission of our sins. In other words, *eis* would denote only that baptism is related somehow to the remission of sins; it would not tell us the nature of that relationship.[162]

(iv) One's view of whether baptism is the means of remission will help to determine how one interprets this verse, not vice versa; to use this verse to support baptismal remission, therefore, is circular reasoning.

(v) " ... the phrase 'for the remission of sins,' used [here], is also used to describe John the Baptist's baptism (Luke 3:3; Mark 1:4), but no one supposes that his baptism literally washed away people's sins (why would they need to later be rebaptized? Cf. Acts 19:1–6)."[163]

(vi) Therefore, it is best to understand "for the remission of your sins" here as denoting not purpose but reference.

e. Water baptism *need not* be by immersion to be effective.

(1) Since baptism is unnecessary for either regeneration or remission, the *mode* of baptism becomes moot in terms of its necessity for salvation. That is, if baptism is not necessary for salvation, then the *mode* of baptism certainly cannot be.

(2) Many Christians who agree with Oneness advocates concerning the mode of baptism (e.g., Baptists) disagree with them about baptism's necessity for salvation, which is the important point at issue here.

(3) However, it is preferable to conclude that baptism need not be performed by immersion.

(a) The most exhaustive study ever done of the Greek words *báptoē* and *baptízoē*, James Wilkinson Dale's four-volume study, demonstrated that they often denote actions having little or nothing to do with immersion.[164] (See also III.D.8.e below.)

---

[161] Ibid., 230.

[162] Robertson, *Word Pictures*, 3:36; *Grammar*, 592, 594–95.

[163] Gregory A. Boyd, "Sharing Your Faith with a Oneness Pentecostal (Part Two)," *Christian Research Journal* (Spring 1991): 7.

[164] See Dale's four-volume study on baptism, which totals over 1,300 pages, listed in the bibliography.

(b) Historical evidence also *does not* support immersion as the only acceptable mode of water baptism in the early church.[165] (See III.D.8.e.(5) below.)

(4) Regardless of one's view on the mode of baptism, it is clear that water baptism is not necessary in order for salvation to occur.

f. Water baptism *need not* be administered with a Jesus' name formula.

(1) Again, if baptism itself is not a necessary condition of salvation, then the words recited at baptism cannot be, either.

(2) However, Scripture nowhere *instructs* recitation of Jesus' name during water baptism. Neither Matthew 1:21 nor Luke 24:47 even refers to water baptism.

(3) While water baptism does symbolize the believer's union with Christ (Rom. 6:3–4; Gal. 3:27), nothing in Scripture commands that such union be signaled by reciting the name of Jesus.

(4) Neither Acts 2:38; 8:16; 10:48; 19:5; 22:16; Romans 6:3–4; Galatians 3:27; Colossians 2:11–12, nor any other passage in Scripture proves that water baptism must be administered with a Jesus' name formula.

(a) The argument confuses narrative (telling what happens) with didactic or doctrinal literature (telling what must be done).

(b) There is no reason to believe the passages convey the very language used in performing water baptism.

(i) None introduces the words of a quotation.

(ii) Romans 6:3–4, Galatians 3:27, and Colossians 2:11–12 don't even use *in the name* but mention instead water baptism "into Christ" or "into his death."

(iii) None of these represent a consistent formula used in water baptism; there are significant differences in wording even among those that mention baptism "in the name" (a ritual formula, in contrast, employs a rigid verbal structure): "in the name of Jesus Christ" (Acts 8:38); "into the name of the Lord Jesus" (Acts 8:16; 19:5); "in the name of Jesus Christ" (Acts 10:48).

(5) Historical evidence does *not* show "that the Jesus' name formula ... was originally used by the early church" or "that the triune formula replaced it only as the church abandoned true monotheism ... and embraced pagan Trinitarianism."

---

[165]Wharton B. Marriott, "Baptism," in *A Dictionary of Christian Antiquities,* eds. William Smith and Samuel Cheetham, 2 vols. (London: John Murray, 1875), 1:168–69.

(a) Citing dictionaries, encyclopedias, and historians does not prove the point because:

   (i) Conflicting authorities may be cited (e.g., Wharton Booth Marriott[166] and J. N. D. Kelly).[167]

   (ii) Specific evidence can justify dissenting from authorities, and good specific evidence exists for early use of a triune formula in baptism. No Christian writings from the first several centuries insist on a Jesus' name formula; none specifically discussing what formula was used even mention a Jesus' name formula as an option; and several important early Christian writings specifically discussing the formula for baptism assert a triune formula (see below).

   (iii) Oneness authors Weisser and Bernard claim that historical evidence supports a Jesus' name formula as original and condemns a triune formula as a later corruption of Christian practice.[168]

However, of the 47 citations they offer, 10 clearly and 3 possibly present no evidence for any formula; 13 clearly and 4 possibly require a triune formula; 11 clearly and 4 possibly accept either formula; and only 4 clearly (including the second-century gnostic Marcionites, who called the Father a false demigod, and two fourth-century Arians and the sixteenth-century Polish Brethren, all of whom denied the deity of Christ) and 3 possibly (including a seventeenth-century Anabaptist who might have denied the deity of Christ; a nineteenth-century Oneness believer; and another nineteenth-century writer who denied the Trinity and may have been Oneness) require a Jesus' name formula.[169]

Of the 23 they cite from the first four centuries, only 3 (the Marcionites and two Arians) require a Jesus' name formula; only 2 clearly and 6 possibly permitted either formula; 6 clearly and 4 possibly required a triune formula; and 6 clearly and 2 possibly present no evidence for any formula.

g. Baptism in the Holy Spirit is *not* essential to salvation, and none of the verses cited by Oneness advocates prove that it is.

   (1) John 3:5 mentions being *born of* the Spirit;

   (2) Romans 8:1–16 mentions the believer's *having* the Spirit as proof that he belongs to Jesus;

---

[166]Ibid., 1:161–62.
[167]J. N. D. Kelly, *Early Christian Doctrines* (New York: Harper & Row, 1960), 89–90.
[168]See Bernard, *Oneness and Trinity*, ch. 8, and Weisser, *Baptism, passim*.
[169]The total here is more than 47 because some are listed as "possibly" supporting more than one position.

(3) Ephesians 1:13–14 calls the Holy Spirit the believer's *"seal"* and "a *deposit* guaranteeing our inheritance";

(4) Titus 3:5 mentions the *renewing* of the Holy Spirit; and

(5) Scripture never equates any of these with being *baptized in* the Spirit.

h. Nothing in Scripture proves that whoever does not speak in tongues is not baptized in the Spirit.

(1) The Bible does not teach that either all converts or all who are baptized in the Spirit speak in tongues.

(a) Luke 11:13 and Acts 2:39 do not equate the *gift of the Spirit* with *conversion/salvation* or connect it inseparably with that.

(b) Mark 16:17 never mentions being baptized in the Spirit (or any synonymous phrases). If Jesus' statement implies that *all* disciples will speak in tongues, then it also implies that *all* "will cast out demons; . . . will take up serpents; and if they drink anything deadly, it will by no means hurt them; . . . will lay hands on the sick, and they will recover" (Mark 16:17–18 NKJV), and hence by Bernard's reasoning whoever does not do *any one of these things* is not baptized in the Spirit and hence not saved, a position Bernard rejects.

(2) The five accounts in Acts, taken singly or together, do not prove that speaking in tongues is the initial evidence of receiving or being baptized in the Spirit.

(a) Acts 2:1–4 does not report the disciples' receiving the Spirit, because they had received him seven weeks before (John 20:22–23).[170]

(b) Even if tongues occurred in all five events (Acts 2:1–4; 8:8, 12–18; 10:44–48; 19:1–7; 19:17), this does not prove that tongues were the invariable evidence of being baptized in the Spirit.

(i) To argue such is to confuse descriptive with prescriptive writing.

(ii) None of these texts, or any others, either explicitly or implicitly state that speaking in tongues is the (or an) indispensable/inevitable sign of being converted or baptized in the Spirit.

(c) In Paul's case (Acts 9:17; see also 1 Cor. 14:18), we need to know not whether Paul ever spoke in tongues, but

(i) Whether he spoke in tongues at his conversion and

---

[170]J. Rodman Williams, *Renewal Theology*, 3 vols. (Grand Rapids: Zondervan, 1988, 1990, 1992), 2:174, 186–88.

    (ii) Whether his speaking in tongues was the indispensable sign of his salvation or baptism in the Spirit.

    (iii) The texts tell us neither, and to assume either is to argue in a circle.

    (iv) According to Oneness Pentecostal teaching, the tongues Paul discusses in 1 Corinthians 12 and 14 differs from the tongues of initial evidence and is not shared by all.[171]

    (v) Therefore, Oneness Pentecostals cannot argue from 1 Corinthians 14:18 that Paul must have spoken in tongues as initial evidence of conversion in Acts 9:17.

(d) Other passages in Acts tell of conversions or of people being baptized or filled with the Spirit but do *not* mention tongues (Acts 2:37–41; 4:31; 6:3–6; 7:55; 11:24; Acts 13:52). So while three passages mentioning people being filled with the Spirit explicitly mention their speaking in tongues (Acts 2:1–4; 10:44–48; 19:1–7), one may imply it (8:8, 12–18), it is a highly debatable inference in one other passage (19:17), and six do not mention it.

(e) Other New Testament figures were filled with (= baptized in) the Spirit, of whom we are never told that they spoke in tongues: Jesus' mother (Luke 1:35); Elizabeth (Luke 1:41); Zacharias (Luke 1:67); John the Baptist (Luke 1:15); Simeon (Luke 2:25–27); Jesus (Matt. 3:16 par. Mark 1:10, Luke 3:22–23, and John 1:32; Luke 4:1, 14, 18; Acts 10:38; compare Isaiah 11:1–2; 42:1–4; 61:1–3).

(f) Many Old Testament figures were filled with (= baptized in) the Spirit (= the Spirit came upon them = fell upon them), of whom we are never told that they spoke in tongues[172] (Ex. 31:3–5; Num. 11:17; 11:25; 11:26; 24:2–3;

---

[171]"The gift of divers kinds of tongues, while similar or the same in sound, is not to be confused with the speaking with tongues which occurs as the initial evidence of the baptism of the Holy Ghost" (Bernard et al., *Meet UPCI*, 101). That Bernard and his coauthors devote six full paragraphs to the point indicates how important it is to them; it is not peripheral and cannot be abandoned without abandoning the "indispensable initial evidence" position, since Paul insists that the gift of tongues he discusses in 1 Cor. 12 and 14 is *not* shared by all (see 1 Cor. 12:29–30). Other Oneness Pentecostal writers make the same point (Reeves, *Holy Ghost*, iii; Jack Visker, *The Baptism of the Holy Spirit* [Hazelwood, Mo.: Word Aflame Press, 1990], 16–17).

[172]Recognizing this is not inconsistent with recognizing a marked difference between the Spirit's activity in the old and new dispensations (Joel 2:28; John 7:39). The Old Testament references to being filled with the Spirit all (except in the case of David, who was in a unique way the precursor of Christ) indicate temporary conditions, while in the New Testament being filled with the Spirit appears to be anticipated as an ongoing condition (although this is not automatic, or Paul would not have *commanded* the Ephesians to "be being filled with the Spirit" [Eph. 5:18, emphasizing the present imperative verb] after having warned them not to "grieve the Holy Spirit of God" [4:30]; see Francis Foulkes, *The Epistle of Paul to the Ephesians* [Grand Rapids: Eerdmans, 1978], 152). Also, the filling of the Spirit in the Old Testament generally came on isolated persons (but not entirely; Samuel's band of prophets apparently all were filled, and when Saul

Judg. 3:10; 6:34; 11:29; 13:25; 14:6, 19; 15:14; 1 Sam. 11:6; 10:5–6; 16:14; 19:23–24; 19:20; 16:13; 2 Sam. 23:1–2; 1 Chron. 12:18; 2 Chron. 20:14–15; 24:20; Mic. 3:8).

(g) So of at least forty distinct passages in the Bible that mention people being filled with (= baptized in, fallen upon by, come upon by, poured upon by, etc.) the Spirit, only three explicitly mention tongues, in only one other can tongues reasonably be inferred, in only one other can tongues be tentatively inferred (and then only by assuming a view of tongues contrary to that of Oneness Pentecostals), and thirty-five do not mention tongues.

(h) Therefore, the Bible does not teach that speaking in tongues is the indispensable result or evidence of being baptized in the Spirit, much less of being converted.

(3) That the apostles recognized tongues as evidence of being filled with the Spirit (Acts 10:46) does not imply that all who were filled spoke in tongues.

(a) Just as while all humans must be mammals, not all mammals must be humans,

(b) so also while all who genuinely speak in tongues must have been baptized in the Spirit, not all who have been baptized in the Spirit must speak in tongues.

D. Arguments for the Biblical Doctrine of Salvation

1. In Adam, all humankind fell into sin, guilt, and spiritual death; therefore, no person can satisfy God's requirements of perfect righteousness or atone for his or her own sin. Agreed. (See Rom. 5:12–19; Ps. 49:7–9.)

2. Salvation is by God's grace through faith in Jesus Christ, who died as a substitutionary sacrifice to satisfy the penalty for human sin. Agreed. (See Rom. 3:28, 4:4–5.)

3. Salvation requires a new birth. Agreed. (See John 3:3, 5–7.)

4. New birth is a gift of God's sovereign grace, independent of the sinner's action (Rom. 9:15–21).

   a. It comes about "through the living and enduring word of God" (1 Peter 1:23; see also James 1:18).

   b. "The wind blows wherever it pleases. You hear its sound, but you cannot tell where it comes from or where it is going. So it is with everyone born of the Spirit" (John 3:8; see vv. 3–8; see also 1 Peter 1:3; John 5:21; 6:44–45, 65).

---

sent messengers to them, they also were filled), while in the New Testament it is widespread among believers. In the Old Testament, it was generally restricted to the Jewish people (but not entirely; Balaam was Gentile), while in the New Testament Gentiles were just as likely to be filled. The differences appear to be of extent and duration, not fundamentally of kind; in every way, the Old Testament anticipates the New.

    c. "Like the rest, we were by nature objects of wrath. But because of his great love for us, God, who is rich in mercy, made us alive with Christ even when we were dead in transgressions—it is by grace you have been saved" (Eph. 2:3b–5).

5. New birth makes God's call effectual.

    a. It is a precondition (John 1:12–13;[173] 3:3, 5; 5:24; 1 John 5:1) of the faith to which we are called and so cannot depend on faith.

    b. "By this divine work the sinner is 'recreated in newness of life' (Murray), has the defilement of his heart cleansed or 'washed' away (Ezek[iel] 36:25–26; John 3:5; Tit[us] 3:5), and is enabled to 'see' and to 'enter' the kingdom of God by faith (John 3:3, 5). He is also enabled to believe in Jesus (John 1:12–13), to believe that Jesus is the Christ (1 John 5:1), to love others, particularly other Christians (1 John 4:7; 5:1); and to do righteousness and to shun the life of sin (1 John 3:9; 5:18)."[174]

6. Faith and repentance follow new birth.

    a. "I tell you the truth, anyone hearing (*akoúōn*, present tense) my word and believing (*pisteúōn*, present tense) him who sent me has (*échei*, present tense) eternal life and does not come (*érchetai*, present tense) into condemnation but has crossed over (*metabébēken*, perfect tense) from death into life" (John 5:24, author's trans.). Crossing over from death into life (regeneration) must have been completed (the import of the perfect tense) before hearing and believing can occur.

    b. It was only after Peter's listeners had been "cut to the heart" so that they asked, "Brothers, what shall we do," that they could repent (Acts 2:37–38), indicating that God had already worked in their hearts before they repented.

    c. Faith and repentance are both gifts from God (Ps. 80:3, 7, 19; Jer. 31:18; Lam. 5:21; Acts 5:31; 11:18; 13:46–48; 18:27; Phil. 1:29; 2 Tim. 2:25).

7. Faith results in justification (Rom. 3:28), which leads to definitive sanctification (God's setting the believer apart to himself), adoption, progressive sanctification (growth in holiness), perseverance in holiness, and glorification (Rom. 8:28–39, esp. vv. 29–30).

    a. Justification is by faith, not by works (Rom. 3:21–30; 4:3–5).

       (1) Negative justification is God's remission of the sinner's guilt and debt for sin (Rom. 4:4–8).

---

[173]Where "right (*exousían*, a legal term) to become children of God" denotes adoption, while "born of God" denotes regeneration. See Robert L. Reymond, *Our "So Great Salvation,"* unpublished class syllabus (St. Louis: Covenant Theological Seminary, n.d.), 107.

[174]Ibid., 116.

(a) Christ paid the judicial debt for the believer's sin by his death on the cross (Matt. 20:28; 1 Tim. 2:6; Titus 2:14; 1 Peter 1:18–19).

(b) Christ's payment (ransom of the believer from condemnation) is credited to the believer (Rom. 5:12–19).

(c) Thus the believer has no liability in God's judgment (Rom. 6:23; 8:1–4).

(2) Positive justification is God's declaration of the sinner as righteous in his judgment.

(a) Christ obeyed the law as the believer's substitute, and his obedience is credited to the believer (Rom. 5:18–19).

(b) Thus, because of his union with Christ, the believer is acceptable in God's judgment (Eph. 1:3–8; 2:1–10, 13, 18).

b. Definitive sanctification is God's setting the believer apart to himself as holy ("saints"), separate from the lost world (Acts 26:18; Eph. 1:1; Phil. 1:1; Col. 1:2).

c. Adoption is the believer's becoming God's child and so an heir with Christ (John 1:12–13; Rom. 8:14–17; Gal. 4:4–5; Eph. 1:4–5, 13–14).

d. Progressive sanctification is the believer's increasingly overcoming sin and living righteously in this life, not by his own strength but by God's work in him through his Word (John 17:17; Rom. 6–7; 8:13; 12:2; 2 Cor. 3:18; 7:1; Eph. 4:11–16; Phil. 2:12–13; Col. 3:5; 1 Thess. 5:23; 1 Peter 2:2).

e. Perseverance in holiness is the believer's continuing steadfast in faith and in progressive sanctification until his death or Christ's return, and it is assured by God's preserving power (Ps. 37:23–24; 73:1–2, 23; John 6:37–40; 10:28–29; Rom. 5:8b–10; 8:30–39; 1 Cor. 1:8–9; 3:15; Phil. 1:6; Heb. 7:25; 1 Peter 1:5).

(1) Some Scriptures warn that only those who do persevere will be saved (Matt. 24:13; John 8:31; 15:6; 1 Cor. 15:1–2; Col. 1:22–23; Heb. 3:6, 14; 10:36, 39).

(a) This warning rebukes the presumption of those who merely *profess* faith but have never been regenerated and therefore do not truly know Christ.

(b) It does not imply that those whom God has regenerated and given faith may not in fact persevere, for their perseverance is ensured by God's faithfulness (Rom. 8:23–39).

(2) Some Scriptures warn that those who apostatize will perish (Rom. 14:15; 1 Cor. 8:11; Heb. 3:6, 14).

(a) True, any who would apostatize would be lost.

(b) But God uses the warning to ensure that none he has called, regenerated, and justified will apostatize (Rom. 8:29–30).

(c) The case is analogous to Acts 27:13–43. God revealed before the shipwreck that none would be lost (vv. 22–25).

Yet Paul warned, "Unless these men stay with the ship, you cannot be saved" (v. 31). In response, the soldiers stayed with the ship (v. 32) and were saved.

(3) Some Scriptures "allegedly affirm ... that Christians who have clearly been in the faith either have fallen, may fall, or shall fall away from the estate of salvation and be finally lost"[175] (Matt. 24:10, 12; 1 Tim. 1:19; 4:1; 2 Tim. 4:10; Heb. 6:4–6; 2 Peter 2:20–22). However:

   (a) Such passages "teach that there is such a thing as 'temporary faith' which is not true faith in Christ at all. . . . In His parable of the sower and the four kinds of soil, Jesus informed His disciples ... that some ... would 'immediately receive [the Word] with joy,' but then, because 'they have no firm root in themselves but are only temporary [*próskairoí*], when affliction or persecution arises because of the Word, immediately they fall away' (Matt[hew] 13:5–6, 20–21; Mark 4:5–6, 16–17)."[176]

   (b) Of such people Scripture itself declares the judgment: "They went out from us, but they did not really belong to us. For if they had belonged to us, they would have remained with us; but their going showed that none of them belonged to us" (1 John 2:19).

(4) These warnings should not undermine the believer's confidence that he will "through faith [be] shielded by God's power until the coming of the salvation that is ready to be revealed in the last time" (1 Peter 1:5; see also Rom. 8:38–39; 2 Tim. 1:12; 1 John 2:3; 3:14; 4:13; 5:13).

   f. Glorification is the certain destiny of all who, having been regenerated, repent and believe in Christ (Rom. 8:17–23, 29–30; 9:22–23; 1 Cor. 15:51–57; 2 Cor. 4:17; 5:8; Eph. 5:25–27; Phil. 1:21–23; 3:21; 2 Thess. 2:14; Heb. 12:23; Rev. 14:13).

   g. Romans 8:28–30 presents the "golden chain" of salvation: the believer's progression to glorification is ensured by God's justifying grace and transforming power.

   "And we know that in all things God works for the good of those who love him, who have been called according to his purpose. For those God foreknew he also predestined to be conformed to the likeness of his Son, that he might be the firstborn among many brothers. And those he predestined, he also called; those he called, he also justified; those he justified, he also glorified" (Rom. 8:28–30).

---

[175]Ibid., 154.
[176]Ibid., 155.

(1) Although believers "work out [their own] salvation" (Phil. 2:12), "it is God who works in [them] to will and to act according to his good purpose" (Phil. 2:13; see also Rom. 8:28), in conformity with which he works everything "in order that we ... might be for the praise of his glory" (Eph. 1:12).

(2) The purpose of God's call in believers is that they should be holy (Eph. 1:4), conformed to the image of his Son (Rom. 8:29).

(3) His call is founded on his predestinating choice (Rom. 8:30).

(4) His predestinating choice is founded on his loving foreknowledge.

   (a) This foreknowledge is not of *facts about* these persons, but of *the persons* themselves (*"those* God foreknew," not "those about whom God foreknew *something*").

   (b) It is not mere intellectual knowing but personal, covenantal knowing comparable to a man's knowing his wife (Gen. 4:1) and Christ's knowing those who are his and not knowing those who are not his (Matt. 7:23).

   (c) The word therefore means "to forelove," to establish beforehand a loving, covenantal relationship.

(5) All who are foreknown (foreloved) are predestined to be conformed to the image of Christ; none are left out (Rom. 8:29).

(6) All who are predestined (and hence all who are foreknown) are called; none are left out (v. 30).

(7) All who are called (and hence all who are predestined and all who are foreknown) are justified; none are left out (v. 30).

(8) All who are justified (and hence all who are called, and all who are predestined, and all who are foreknown) are glorified; none are left out (v. 30).

(9) With this knowledge the believer receives blessed assurance of his never-ending security in God's gracious love: "... If God is for us, who can be against us? ... Who shall separate us from the love of Christ? ... I am convinced that neither death nor life, neither angels nor demons, neither the present nor the future, nor any powers, neither height nor depth, nor *anything else in all creation*, will be able to separate us from the love of God that is in Christ Jesus our Lord" (Rom. 8:31–39 [emphasis added]).

8. In this saving process, water baptism is a sign and seal (outward stamp of God's ownership of the believer), made effectual as such through faith, of the believer's union with Christ and his cleansing from sin; its absence cannot condemn the believer; its mode is flexible; its proper formula is triune.

a. Water baptism signifies and seals the believer's union with Christ, but also with the Father and the Holy Spirit.

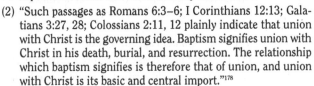

(1) "We must take our point of departure from the very formula which Jesus used in the institution, 'baptising them into the name of the Father, and of the Son, and of the Holy Spirit' (Matt[hew] 28:19). It is this notion of 'baptising into' that must be appreciated and analysed. This formula appears in other connections, as, for example, 'baptised into Moses' (I Cor[inthians] 10:2) and 'baptised into the name of Paul' (I Cor[inthians] 1:13). It is apparent that it expresses a relationship to the person into whom or into whose name persons may have been baptised. It is this fact of relationship that is basic."[177]

(2) "Such passages as Romans 6:3–6; I Corinthians 12:13; Galatians 3:27, 28; Colossians 2:11, 12 plainly indicate that union with Christ is the governing idea. Baptism signifies union with Christ in his death, burial, and resurrection. The relationship which baptism signifies is therefore that of union, and union with Christ is its basic and central import."[178]

(3) It is significant, in light of this, that those who insist on a Jesus' name formula always reject the doctrine of the Trinity. There is a clear connection between one's view of God and one's view of the meaning and formula of water baptism.

b. Water baptism signifies and seals the believer's purification from sin.

(1) "There does not appear to be in the New Testament any passage which expressly says that baptism represents purification from the defilement of sin, that is to say, regeneration. But since baptism is washing with water, since it involves a religious use of water, and since regeneration is expressed elsewhere in terms of washing (John 3:5; Titus 3:5; I Cor. 6:11), it is difficult, if not impossible, to escape the conclusion that this washing with water involved in baptism represents that indispensable purification which is presupposed in union with Christ and without which [namely, the purification, not the water baptism] no one can enter into the kingdom of God.

(2) "There is also the consideration that baptism is the circumcision of the New Testament (Col. 2:11, 12). Circumcision, without doubt, symbolised purification from defilement. We should infer that baptism does also.

(3) ".... John's baptism did have reference to the forgiveness of sins (Matt. 3:6; Mark 1:4; Luke 3:3). We should expect that such a reference could not be excluded from the import of

[177]Murray, *Baptism*, 3.
[178]Ibid.

Christian baptism. Such an expectation is confirmed by express intimation in other passages; Christian baptism stands in a similar relation to the remission of sins (Acts 2:38; 22:16; I Peter 3:21).

(4) "We may therefore conclude that baptism represents the remission of our sin or, in other words, purification from the guilt of sin by the sprinkling of the blood of Christ."[179]

c. Water baptism is made effectual as a sign of union with Father, Son, and Spirit, and as a sign of purification from sin, only through faith (John 3:18; Heb. 11:6).

d. The absence of water baptism does not condemn the believer, for "Whoever believes in him is not condemned" (John 3:18) and "whoever believes in him shall not perish but have eternal life" (John 3:16).

e. The mode of water baptism is flexible.

(1) The word itself does not require any particular mode.

(2) The reference to a ritual washing of the hands as a baptism shows that it sometimes involved pouring (Matt. 15:2; Mark 7:2–5; Luke 11:38), for early Jewish sources show that this ritual involved pouring water over the hands, not immersing the hands into a basin of water.[180]

(3) The fact that various Old Testament ritual sprinklings (Heb. 9:13, 19, 21) are called baptisms (see Heb. 9:10, where the NIV has *washings* for Gk. *baptismoîs*) shows that it sometimes involved sprinkling.

(4) That it might sometimes have involved immersion is seen from the use of *baptízō* to translate the Hebrew *tabal* in 2 Kings 5:14, which says that Naaman "dipped (Heb. *tabal*; Gk. *baptízō*) himself in the Jordan seven times."

(5) The early church was flexible as to the mode of baptism.

(a) One of the earliest noncanonical Christian documents, the *Didache*, says of the mode of baptism: "But concerning baptism, thus shall ye baptize. Having first recited all these things, baptize in the name of the Father and of the Son and of the Holy Spirit in living (running) water. But if thou hast not living water, then baptize in other water; and if thou art not able in cold, then in warm. But if thou hast neither, then pour water on the head thrice in the name of the Father and of the Son and of the Holy Spirit. . . ."[181]

---

[179]Ibid., 4–5.

[180]Ibid., 12–14; Alfred Edersheim, *The Life and Times of Jesus the Messiah*, 3d ed. (Grand Rapids: Eerdmans, 1971), 2:10–12.

[181]*Didache*, 7:1–3; in Lightfoot and Harmer, *Apostolic Fathers*, 232.

(b) Cyprian, a third-century bishop of Carthage, asked whether sprinkling or pouring were legitimate modes of baptism, responded that he knew of no prior official ruling on such a question by the church; that "the mode in which the water was applied was a matter of minor importance";[182] and "that the sprinkling also of water prevails equally with the washing of salvation; and that when this is done in the Church, where the faith both of receiver and giver is sound, all things hold and may be consummated and perfected by the majesty of the Lord and by the truth of faith."[183]

f. The proper formula for water baptism is triune.

(1) Jesus prescribed this formula in Matthew 28:19—"baptizing them in the name of the Father and of the Son and of the Holy Spirit." There are good reasons to take this as prescribing a formula:

(a) It appears as the finale of Matthew's narrative of the life and teachings of Jesus.

(b) It is part of Christ's parting discourse.

(c) Its rhythmic form makes it ideal for memorization and ritual use.[184]

(2) The early church used a triune formula.

(a) The *Didache* 7:1–3 expressly prescribed it.

(b) Justin Martyr, in the second century, said it was the common practice of the churches (*First Apology* 61:3, 10–13).[185]

(c) Irenaeus, in the second century, wrote, "We received baptism for the remission of sins in the name of God the Father, and in the name of Jesus Christ, the Son of God, Who was incarnate and died and rose again, and in the Holy Spirit of God."[186]

(d) Tertullian, in the second century, wrote of "the formula prescribed" by Jesus as "baptizing them into the name of the Father, and of the Son, and of the Holy Spirit."[187]

(e) Cyprian, in the third century, condemned those who rejected the triune formula and baptized "only in the name of Jesus Christ," insisting instead that baptism must be "in the name of the Father, and of the Son, and of the Holy

---

[182]Marriott, "Baptism," 1:168–69.

[183]Cyprian, *Epistle* LXXV.12, in *ANF*, 5:401.

[184]See E. Calvin Beisner, "God in Three Persons: The Doctrine of the Trinity in the New Testament and the Nicene Creed" (Bachelor's thesis, University of Southern California, 1978), 34 n. 7.

[185]*ANF*, 1:183.

[186]*Dem.* 3, cited in Kelly, *Early*, 90.

[187]Tertullian, *On Baptism*, xiii, in *ANF*, 3:676; compare *Against Praxeas*, xvi, in *ANF*, 3:623.

71

Ghost" according to Christ's command, "in the full and united Trinity."[188]

(f) Augustine, in the early fifth century, wrote, "you will more easily find heretics who do not baptize at all, than any who baptize without" the words of the triune formula.[189]

(g) The church historian Sozomen, in the fifth century, wrote of the triune formula as "the apostolical tradition which has been carefully handed down to the present day" and of the insistence on a Jesus' name formula as an "innovation" brought on by fourth-century Arians (who denied the deity of Christ).[190] Writing in the early fifth century, the church historian Socrates agreed.[191]

[188]Cyprian, *Epistle* 72 (73, according to the Oxford edition), in *ANF*, 5:383.

[189]Augustine, *On Baptism, Against the Donatists*, vi.25, compare iii.14–15; in *NPNF*, 1, 4:442, 491.

[190]Sozomen, *Ecclesiastical History*, vi.26; in *NPNF*, 2, 2:363.

[191]Socrates, *Ecclesiastical History*, v.25, in *NPNF*, 2, 2:135.

Part III: Witnessing Tips

I. Tactical Suggestions[1]

A. Demonstrate Love and Concern

As one of their own former adherents states, "The most problematic aspect of my theology when I was a Oneness Pentecostal was the belief that no one other than us Oneness Pentecostals was going to heaven. Trinitarian Christians simply were not saved! So every time I met Trinitarian Christians who clearly reflected the loving presence of Jesus in their lives by the way they related to me, I confronted more strong evidence that my theology could not be true."[2]

B. Show Common Ground

1. Since one strong point of Oneness Pentecostal soteriology is its insistence that conversion bear fruit in a changed life, express your own sorrow that many people who claim to be Christians do not live like Christians.

2. Often Oneness Pentecostals observe people who claim to be Christians neglecting Scripture and living unholy lives. This understandably turns them off to much of "evangelical Christianity."

3. Demonstrate in your own life that you revere Scripture and strive for holy living.

C. Focus on Their Weakest Points

1. "Like other authoritarian doctrinal systems, Oneness Pentecostal theology pretty much stands or falls as a whole in the minds of its followers. If you can show it to be in error at all, even on a peripheral point, you have gone a long way toward undermining their trust in the entire doctrinal system which holds them in bondage."[3]

2. Some of their weakest points include

   a. Speaking in tongues as necessary to salvation (see Part II: Theology, III.C.4.g–h above);

      (1) "Oneness Pentecostals believe that unless one has spoken in tongues, one does not *have* the Holy Spirit (not just the *fullness* of the Holy Spirit, as certain other Pentecostals hold).

---

[1] I am indebted to Gregory A. Boyd, a former Oneness Pentecostal, for some of the insights here. See his "Sharing Your Faith with a Oneness Pentecostal (Part One)," *Christian Research Journal* (Winter 1991): 7; and "Sharing Your Faith with a Oneness Pentecostal (Part Two)," *Christian Research Journal* (Spring 1991): 7.

[2] Boyd, "Sharing Your Faith ... (Part One)," 7.

[3] Ibid.

(2) "And, since a person cannot be saved without the Holy Spirit (Rom. 8:9), it follows that only those who have spoken in tongues are truly saved....

(3) "The Oneness Pentecostal position frequently results in sincere believers 'seeking for the Holy Ghost' for days, weeks, and even years. (I've seen some die yet seeking!) These poor souls are literally begging God to save them. The reason they do not receive the Holy Spirit, and hence salvation, is presumably because they lack sufficient faith, or they have unacknowledged sin in their lives.

(4) "In a loving way, ask Oneness Pentecostals if they have ever wondered why there is no biblical precedent for this sad phenomenon. (I assure you, they have!) Why is salvation so 'easy' in the Bible?

(5) "And if sinners must first believe 'sufficiently' and cleanse themselves 'sufficiently' in order to receive (as a reward?) the Holy Spirit, why does the New Testament portray faith and sanctification as the *result,* not the basis, of receiving the Holy Spirit (1 Cor. 12:3; Rom. 15:16; 2 Thess. 2:13)?"[4]

    b. Their denial that Jesus existed as the Son of God before the incarnation (see Part II: Theology, I.C.4 and I.D.3 above);

    c. Identifying Jesus himself as God the Father and the Holy Spirit (see Part II: Theology, II.C.1.b–e and II.D.2.e–i above); and

    d. Their insistence that baptism is necessary for salvation and must be by immersion and "in Jesus' name" (see Part II: Theology, III.C.4.c–g above).

II. Focus on Major Issues of Christology, Theology, and Soteriology.

A. General Observations

1. Many Oneness Pentecostal beliefs and practices (particularly parts of their "holiness code") are strange and legalistic and lack biblical ground, but most of these are not at the heart of Oneness Pentecostal doctrine and will be forsaken as a former adherent begins to enjoy his true liberty in Christ.[5]

2. Therefore, do not be distracted from the most important questions, which include: Who is Jesus? Who are the Father, the Son, and the Holy Spirit? What must I do to be saved?

---

[4]Ibid.

[5]See David M. Wasmundt, *Neo Phariseeism: An Inside Look at Hairsplitting Theologies* (Chapel Hill, N.C.: Professional Press, 1992).

B. On Christology

1. Point out the strong evidence that Jesus existed as the Son of God before the incarnation.

2. Point out that the title *Son of God* properly applies to him not only as man but also as God (see Part II: Theology, I.D.3; use Col. 1:12–16; Heb. 1:1–8).

C. On the Trinity

1. Point out the lack of biblical evidence that Jesus is the Father or the Holy Spirit, and the abundance of biblical evidence that these Persons are distinct (see Part II: Theology, II.C.1.b–e and II.D.2.e–i above; use John 8:54–58; 14:15–17, 26; 15:26).

2. A former UPCI pastor points out that " ... while Jesus is never once explicitly called 'Father' in the New Testament, He is explicitly referred to as 'the Son' (of God, of man, etc.) over 200 times. What is more, the Father is referred to as distinct from Jesus the Son throughout the New Testament over 200 times. And over 50 times, Jesus the Son and the Father are juxtaposed within the same verse. Ask your Oneness friend why there is this overwhelming (indeed, unanimous) emphasis on Jesus' being the Son of God and being distinct from the Father if in fact Scripture also wants to teach us that Jesus is *Himself* the Father? Why is Scripture so clear on the first point and yet so silent on the second?"[6]

D. On Soteriology

1. Point out that salvation is by grace alone through faith alone rather than by any human effort (see Part II: Theology, III.C.4.a–h and III.D.4–8 above; use John 3:16, 18; 5:24; Rom. 3:28; Titus 3:5).

2. Point out that just as in the Old Testament justification sometimes preceded circumcision, the sign and seal of covenantal union with God and of purification from sin (Rom. 4:9–13), so in the New Testament justification sometimes precedes baptism, the new sign and seal (Col. 2:11–12) of covenantal union with God and of purification from sin (e.g., Acts 10:44–48), so that in both Testaments "the promise comes by faith, so that it may be by grace and may be guaranteed to all Abraham's offspring—not only to those who are of the law but also to those who are of the faith of Abraham. He is the father of us all. ... This is why '[his faith] was credited to him as righteousness.' The words 'it was credited to him' were written not for him alone, but also for us, to whom God will credit righteousness—for us who believe in him who raised Jesus our Lord from the dead" (Rom. 4:16, 22–24).

3. Point out that in the New Testament it is not outward baptism with water that saves but "the pledge of a good conscience toward God. It saves you by the resurrection of Jesus Christ" (1 Peter 3:21), just as

---

[6]Boyd, "Sharing Your Faith ... (Part Two)," 7.

in the Old Testament it was not outward circumcision that saved but "circumcision of the heart, by the Spirit, not by the written code" (Rom. 2:29; see also 2:28), not "done by the hands of men but ... by Christ" (Col. 2:11; see also 2:10–12).

4. Point out the inconsistency between claiming that salvation is by faith alone and yet claiming that water baptism is necessary for salvation (Titus 3:5).

III. Correct Their False Notions of Evangelical Trinitarianism.

A. By Expressing Orthodox Beliefs Accurately

1. Generally speaking, be careful that you express orthodox beliefs accurately so as not to perpetuate common misconceptions.

2. On Christology, study the Chalcedonian Creed (see Part II: Theology, I.D.1 above) to ensure that you can accurately state orthodox Christology.

3. On the Trinity, study the Athanasian Creed (see Part: II, Theology, II.D.1 above) to ensure that you can accurately state orthodox Trinitarianism.

4. On soteriology, study one of the great Protestant confessions; the *Westminster Confession*, one of the most widely accepted, would be very effective.[7]

B. By Correcting Their False Notions of Evangelical Christology

1. Stress that you believe that Jesus Christ is fully God (John 1:1; Titus 2:13), since most Oneness Pentecostals believe that Trinitarians think Christ is less than fully God.

2. Stress that you believe that all the fullness of the Godhead dwells bodily in the incarnate Jesus (Col. 2:9), since most Oneness Pentecostals believe that Trinitarians think only part of God was incarnate in Christ.

C. By Correcting Their False Notions of the Trinity

1. Stress that you believe in the existence of only one God (Deut. 4:35; 6:4; 1 Tim. 2:5), since many Oneness Pentecostals believe that Trinitarians think the Father, the Son, and the Holy Spirit are three different Gods.

2. Stress that by saying that Father, Son, and Spirit are distinct Persons, you do not mean that they are like distinct human beings, with bodies and each constituting only *part* of humanity, but that they are dis-

---

[7]Philip Schaff, *The Creeds of Christendom,* 3 vols. (Grand Rapids: Baker, 1977), 3:600–673. For a thorough study of the confession, see G. I. Williamson, *The Westminster Confession of Faith for Study Classes* (Philadelphia: Presbyterian & Reformed, 1964).

tinct self-conscious agents, each of whom is fully God and subsists as the whole, undivided nature of God.

D. By Correcting Their False Notions of Evangelical Soteriology

1. Against the Oneness Pentecostal stereotype of evangelicals as antinomians (i.e., people who reject the law of God and live disobediently), insist that real faith bears fruit in a life of holy obedience (Rom. 6; Eph. 1:4; 2:8–10; 4:1; 1 Thess. 2:10–12).

2. Against the image of evangelicals as having a careless attitude about water baptism,

   a. Insist that willful rejection of baptism is sinful disobedience that may very well indicate rejection of Christ's authority and so lack of salvation (Matt. 7:21–23; Acts 2:37–38), and

   b. Point out that water baptism is an important part of the discipling process and asserts Christ's authority over his people (Matt. 28:18–20).

3. Against the image of evangelicals who believe that their security in salvation means they can persist in living in unrepentant sin without fear of damnation,

   a. Assure them that real conversion brings real fruit (Matt. 7:17–20);

   b. Insist that mere profession of faith is not proof of real conversion (Matt. 7:21–23);

   c. Affirm that only those who endure to the end will be saved (Matt. 10:22; 24:13; Mark 4:1–20; 13:13); and

   d. Remind them, nonetheless, that Scripture asserts that those who do not endure to the end were never converted in the first place (1 John 2:19).

Part IV:
Selected Bibliography

Although many more works were consulted in preparing to write this book, space permits listing here only those cited.

I. Sources Written by Oneness Pentecostals

Bernard, David K. *Essentials of the New Birth*. Hazelwood, Mo.: Word Aflame Press, 1987.

_____. *In the Name of Jesus*. Hazelwood, Mo.: Word Aflame Press, 1992.

_____. *Oneness and Trinity* A.D. *100–300: The Doctrine of God in Ancient Christian Writings*. Hazelwood, Mo.: Word Aflame Press, 1991.

_____. *The Oneness of God*. Hazelwood, Mo.: Word Aflame Press, 1983.

Bernard, David, C. A. Brewer, and P. D. Buford. *Meet the United Pentecostal Church International*. Hazelwood, Mo.: Word Aflame Press, 1989.

Chalfant, William B. *Ancient Champions of Oneness: A History of the True Church of Jesus Christ*. Junction City, Kans., 1979.

Clanton, Charles, Crawford Coon, and Paul Dugas. *Bible Doctrines: Foundation of the Church*. Hazelwood, Mo.: Word Aflame Press, 1984.

Clanton, Charles, Dennis Croucher, and Paul Dugas. *Salvation: Key to Eternal Life*. Hazelwood, Mo.: Word Aflame Press, 1985.

Fauss, Oliver F. *Baptism in God's Plan*. Hazelwood, Mo.: Word Aflame Press, 1990.

Graves, Robert Brent. *The God of Two Testaments*. N.p., 1977.

Hall, J. L. *The United Pentecostal Church and the Evangelical Movement*. Hazelwood, Mo.: Word Aflame Press, 1990.

Magee, Gordon. *Is Jesus in the Godhead or Is the Godhead in Jesus?* Hazelwood, Mo.: Word Aflame Press, 1988.

Paterson, John. *God in Christ Jesus*. Hazelwood, Mo.: Word Aflame Press, 1966.

Reeves, Kenneth V. *The Godhead*. 7th rev. ed. Granite City, Ill.: Inspirational Books and Tapes, 1962.

_____. *The Holy Ghost with Tongues*. 2d ed. Granite City, Ill.: Inspirational Tapes and Books, 1991.

Reynolds, Ralph V. *Truth Shall Triumph: A Study of Pentecostal Doctrines*. Hazelwood, Mo.: Word Aflame Press, 1965.

Rugger, Gary C. *Oneness, Trinity, Arian: Which One Does Scripture Teach?* Bakersfield, Calif.: Sarah's Christian Books, 1988.

Visker, Jack. *The Baptism of the Holy Spirit.* Hazelwood, Mo.: Word Aflame Press, 1990.

Weisser, Thomas. *Jesus' Name Baptism Through the Centuries.* N.p., 1989. (Available from Word Aflame Press.)

Welch, D. L. *Contending for the Faith.* Hazelwood, Mo.: Word Aflame Press, 1988.

Williams, Carl E. *The Bible Plan of Salvation.* Hazelwood, Mo.: Word Aflame Press, 1988.

II. Sources About Oneness Pentecostalism by Outsiders

Boyd, Gregory A. "Sharing Your Faith with a Oneness Pentecostal (Part One)." *Christian Research Journal* (Winter 1991): 7.

_____. "Sharing Your Faith with a Oneness Pentecostal (Part Two)." *Christian Research Journal* (Spring 1991): 7.

Grady, Lee. "Dispute Causes Upheaval in UPC." *Charisma* (May 1933): 76–77.

Wasmundt, David M. *Neo Phariseeism: An Inside Look at Hairsplitting Theologies.* Chapel Hill, N.C.: Professional Press, 1992. (Available from the author, a former UPCI pastor.)

III. Commentaries

Barnes, Albert. *Barnes' Notes on the New Testament.* Edited by Ingram Cobbin. Grand Rapids: Kregel, 1976.

Calvin, John. *Commentary on the Epistles of Paul the Apostle to the Corinthians.* Translated by John Pringle. Vol. 20 of *Calvin's Commentaries.* 1848. Reprint. Grand Rapids: Baker, 1984.

Foulkes, Francis. *The Epistle of Paul to the Ephesians.* Grand Rapids: Eerdmans, 1978.

Jamieson, Robert, A. R. Fausset, and David Brown. *A Commentary, Critical, Experimental, and Practical on the Old and New Testaments.* 3 vols. Reprint. Grand Rapids: Eerdmans, 1976.

Lenski, R. C. H. *The Interpretation of St. John's Gospel.* Minneapolis: Augsburg, 1961.

Lightfoot, J. B. *St. Paul's Epistles to the Colossians and to Philemon.* 1879. Reprint. Grand Rapids: Zondervan, 1974.

Robertson, A. T. *Word Pictures in the New Testament.* 6 vols. Nashville: Broadman, 1932.

Westcott, B. F. *The Gospel According to St. John.* 1881. Reprint. Grand Rapids: Eerdmans, 1991.

IV. Language Helps

Bauer, Walter. *A Greek-English Lexicon of the New Testament and Other Early Christian Literature.* Translated by William F. Arndt and F. Wilbur Gingrich. Revised by F. Wilbur Gingrich and Frederick W. Danker. 2d ed. Chicago: University of Chicago Press, 1979.

Brown, Colin, ed. *The New International Dictionary of New Testament Theology.* 4 vols. Grand Rapids: Zondervan, 1975–85.

Colwell, E. Cadman. "A Definite Rule for the Use of the Article in the Greek New Testament." *Journal of Biblical Literature* 52 (1933): 12–21.

Dale, James W. *Christic and Patristic Baptism: An Inquiry into the Meaning of the Word as Determined by the Usage of the Holy Scriptures and Patristic Writers.* 1874. Reprint. Phillipsburg, N.J.: Presbyterian & Reformed; Wauconda, Ill.: Bolchazy-Carducci; and Toney, Ala.: Loewe Belfort Projects, 1995.

_____. *Classic Baptism: An Inquiry into the Meaning of the Word as Determined by the Usage of Classical Greek Writers.* 1867. Reprint. Phillipsburg, N.J.: Presbyterian and Reformed; Wauconda, Ill.: Bolchazy-Carducci, 1989.

_____. *Johannic Baptism: An Inquiry into the Meaning of the Word as Determined by the Usage of the Holy Scriptures.* 1898. Reprint. Phillipsburg, N.J.: Presbyterian and Reformed; Wauconda, Ill.: Bolchazy-Carducci; and Huntsville, Ala.: Loewe Belfort Projects, 1993.

_____. *Judaic Baptism: An Inquiry into the Meaning of the Word as Determined by the Usage of Jewish and Patristic Writers.* 1869. Reprint. Phillipsburg, N.J.: Presbyterian and Reformed; Wauconda, Ill.: Bolchazy-Carducci; and Huntsville, Ala.: Loewe Belfort Projects, 1991.

Dana, H. E., and Julius R. Mantey. *A Manual Grammar of the Greek New Testament.* 1927. Reprint. New York: Macmillan, 1955.

Harner, Philip B. "Qualitative Anarthrous Predicate Nouns: Mark 15:39 and John 1:1." *Journal of Biblical Literature* 92 (1973): 75–87.

Kuehne, C. "The Greek Article and the Doctrine of Christ's Deity." *Journal of Theology: Church of the Lutheran Confession* 13, no. 3 (September 1973): 12–28; 13, no. 4 (December 1973): 14–30; 14, no. 1 (March 1974): 12–20; 14, no. 2 (June 1974): 16–25; 14, no. 3 (September 1974): 21–33; 14, no. 4 (December 1974): 8–19; 15, no. 1 (March 1975): 8–22.

Liddell, Henry G., and Robert Scott, comps. *A Greek-English Lexicon.* Revised by Henry S. Jones and Roderick McKenzie et al. 9th ed. Oxford: Oxford University Press, 1940.

Metzger, Bruce M. *The Text of the New Testament.* 2d ed. Oxford: Oxford University Press, 1968.

_____. *A Textual Commentary on the Greek New Testament.* New York: United Bible Societies, 1971.

Moulton, James H., and George Milligan. *The Vocabulary of the Greek New Testament.* 1930. Reprint. Grand Rapids: Eerdmans, 1976.

Robertson, A. T. *A Grammar of the Greek New Testament in the Light of Historical Research.* Nashville: Broadman, 1934.

Smith, J. B. *Greek-English Concordance to the New Testament.* Scottdale, Pa.: Herald Press, 1955.

Turner, Nigel. *Syntax.* Vol. 3 of James H. Moulton, *A Grammar of New Testament Greek.* 4 vols. Edinburgh: T. & T. Clark, 1963.

Winer, George B. *A Grammar of the Idiom of the New Testament.* 7th ed. Andover: Warren F. Draper, 1881.

V. Dictionaries and Encyclopedias

Burgess, Stanley M., Gary B. McGee, and Patrick H. Alexander, eds. *Dictionary of Pentecostal and Charismatic Movements.* Grand Rapids: Zondervan, 1988.

Smith, William, and Samuel Cheetham, eds. *A Dictionary of Christian Antiquities.* 2 vols. London: John Murray, 1875.

VI. Patristic Sources

Leloir, Louis, ed. and trans. *St. Éphrem, Commentaire de L'Évangile Concordant, Version Arménienne.* Corpus Scriptorum Christianorum Orientalium, vol. 145. Louvain: Imprimerie Orientalist, L. Durbecq, 1954.

Lightfoot, J. B., ed. and trans. *The Apostolic Fathers: Clement, Ignatius, and Polycarp, Revised Texts with Introductions, Notes, Dissertations, and Translations.* 5 vols. Reprint. Peabody, Mass.: Hendrickson, 1989.

Lightfoot, J. B., and J. R. Harmer, trans. *The Apostolic Fathers: Revised Greek Texts with Introductions and English Translations.* Reprint. Grand Rapids: Baker, 1984.

Plooij, D. *A Primitive Text of the Diatessaron: The Liège Manuscript of a Mediæval Dutch Translation, A Preliminary Study.* Leyden: A. W. Sijthoff's Uitgeversmaatschappij, 1923.

Roberts, Alexander, and James Donaldson, eds. *The Ante-Nicene Fathers: Translations of the Writings of the Fathers down to A.D. 325.* 10 vols. Reprint. Grand Rapids: Eerdmans, 1975.

Schaff, Philip, ed. *Nicene and Post-Nicene Fathers of the Christian Church.* 28 vols. Second Series. Reprint. Grand Rapids: Eerdmans, 1978.

VII. Systematic Theologies

Hodge, Charles. *Systematic Theology.* 3 vols. Grand Rapids: Eerdmans, 1973.

Williams, J. Rodman. *Renewal Theology.* 3 vols. Grand Rapids: Zondervan, 1988, 1990, 1992.

VIII. Histories of Theology

Bethune-Baker, J. F. *An Introduction to the Early History of Christian Doctrine to the Time of the Council of Chalcedon.* London: Methuen and Company, 1903.

Kelly, J. N. D. *Early Christian Doctrines.* New York: Harper & Row, 1960.

Schaff, Philip. *The Creeds of Christendom.* 3 vols. Grand Rapids: Baker, 1977.

IX. Works on the Doctrine of the Trinity and Christology

Except for Anselm's work, only modern works are listed below. Works by the church fathers, included in the *Ante-Nicene Fathers* and the *Nicene and Post-Nicene Fathers* sets, are cited in footnotes.

Anselm of Canterbury. *Cur Deus Homo?* In *A Scholastic Miscellany: Anselm to Ockham,* edited by Eugene R. Fairweather. Library of Christian Classics. Philadelphia: Westminster, 1956.

Beisner, E. Calvin. "God in Three Persons: The Doctrine of the Trinity in the New Testament and the Nicene Creed." Bachelor's thesis, University of Southern California, 1978.

Beisner, E. Calvin. *God in Three Persons.* Wheaton, Ill.: Tyndale House, 1984.

Fortman, Edmund J. *The Triune God: A Historical Study of the Doctrine of the Trinity.* Grand Rapids: Baker, 1982.

Warfield, Benjamin B. "Trinity," in *The International Standard Bible Encyclopedia.* Edited by James Orr et al. 5 vols. Grand Rapids: Eerdmans, 1956. Reprint. 4 vols. Peabody, Mass.: Hendrickson, 1994.

X. Other Sources

Adams, Jay E. *The Meaning and Mode of Baptism.* Phillipsburg, N.J.: Presbyterian and Reformed, 1975.

Beisner, E. Calvin. "The Omniscience of God: Biblical Doctrine and Answers to Objections." *Crosswinds* 2, no. 1 (Spring/Summer 1993): 10–26.

Edersheim, Alfred. *The Life and Times of Jesus the Messiah.* 3d ed. Grand Rapids: Eerdmans, 1971.

Murray, John. *Christian Baptism.* Phillipsburg, N.J.: Presbyterian and Reformed, 1980.

Reymond, Robert L. "Our 'So Great Salvation'." Covenant Theological Seminary, St. Louis. Unpublished class syllabus.

Robinson, John A. T. *Redating the New Testament.* Philadelphia: Westminster, 1976.

Part V:
Parallel Comparison Chart

"Jesus Only" Churches	The Bible

The Doctrine of Christ

"... the [title] Son always refers to the Incarnation and we cannot use it in the absence of the human element" (Bernard, *Oneness of God*, 103).

"... we can only use the term 'Son of God' correctly when it includes the humanity of Jesus" (Bernard, *Oneness of God*, 99).

"The Sonship began at Bethlehem. The Incarnation was the time when the Sonship began.... Here [in Luke 1:35] it is clearly revealed that the humanity of the Lord Jesus is the Son" (Magee, *Is Jesus*, 32).

"We cannot say that God died, so we cannot say 'God the Son' died. On the other hand, we can say that the Son of God died because Son refers to humanity" (Bernard, *Oneness of God*, 100).

"In the past God spoke to our forefathers through the prophets at many times and in various ways, but in these last days he has spoken to us by his Son, ... through whom he made the universe" (Heb. 1:1–2).

"... the Father ... brought us into the kingdom of the Son he loves.... He [the Son] is the image of the invisible God, the firstborn over all creation. For by him [the Son] all things were created ..." (Col. 1:12–16).

"Be shepherds of the church of God, which he bought with his own blood" (Acts 20:28).

"'I am the Alpha and the Omega,' says the Lord God, 'who is, and who was, and who is to come, the Almighty'" (Rev. 1:8). "I am the First and the Last. I am the Living One; I was dead, and behold I am alive for ever and ever!" (Rev. 1:17–18). "These are the words of him who is the First and the Last, who died and came to life again" (Rev. 2:8). "[Jesus said,] 'I am the Alpha and the Omega, the First and the Last, the Beginning and the End'" (Rev. 22:13).

The Doctrine of the Trinity

"... Jesus Himself taught that He was the Father" (Bernard, *Oneness of God*, 67).

"If there is only one God and that God is the Father (Malachi 2:10), and if Jesus is God, then it logically follows that Jesus is the Father" (Bernard, *Oneness of God*, 66).

"The Holy Spirit is the Spirit that was incarnated in Jesus and is Jesus in Spirit form ..." (Bernard, *Oneness and Trinity*, 10).

"If I testify about myself, my testimony is not valid. There is another who testifies in my favor, and I know that his testimony about me is valid.... And the Father who sent me has himself testified concerning me" (John 5:31–32, 37).

"In your own Law it is written that the testimony of two men is valid. I am one who testifies for myself; my other witness is the Father, who sent me" (John 8:17–18).

"Father, the time has come. Glorify your Son, that your Son may glorify you.... And now, Father, glorify me in your presence with the glory I had with you before the world began" (John 17:1, 5).

"... I will ask the Father, and he will give you *another* Counselor to be with you forever—the Spirit of truth" (John 14:16–17, italics added).

"When the Counselor comes, whom *I* will send to you from the Father, the Spirit of truth who goes out from the Father, *he* will testify about *me*" (John 15:26, italics added).

"But when he, the Spirit of truth, comes, he will guide you into all truth. He will not speak on his own; he will speak only what he hears, and he will tell you what is yet to come. He will bring glory to me by taking from what is mine and making it known to you. All that belongs to the Father is mine. That is why I said the Spirit will take from what is mine and make it known to you" (John 16:13–15).

"The oneness of God is not a mystery. . . . The triune nature of God is an incomprehensible mystery" (Bernard, *Oneness and Trinity*, 14).

"Beyond all question, the mystery of godliness is great: He appeared in a body, was vindicated by the Spirit, was seen by angels, was preached among the nations, was believed on in the world, was taken up in glory" (1 Tim. 3:16; see 1 Cor. 4:1; Col. 2:2).

"In the beginning was the Word, and the Word was with God, and the Word was God. . . . In him was life, and that life was the light of men. The light shines in the darkness, but the darkness has not understood it. . . . The true light that gives light to every man was coming into the world. He was in the world, and though the world was made through him, the world did not recognize him. . . .

"No one has ever seen God, but God the One and Only, who is at the Father's side, has made him known" (John 1:1, 4–5, 9–10, 18).[1]

The Doctrine of Salvation

"Water baptism is a part of that process by which a man is born into, or made a part of, the kingdom of God" (Clanton et al., *Bible Doctrines*, 79).

"But when the kindness and love of God our Savior appeared, he saved us, not because of righteous things we had done, but because of his mercy. He saved us through the washing of rebirth and renewal by the Holy Spirit, whom he poured out on us generously through Jesus Christ our Savior, so that, having been justified by his grace, we might become heirs having the hope of eternal life" (Titus 3:4–7).

---

[1]The Greek word *mustērion* may denote something too profound to be understood by human reason, or something once hidden but then revealed by God (Bauer, *Lexicon*, 530–31). That the doctrine of the Trinity is a mystery is entirely consistent with what Scripture reveals about the incomprehensible, yet revealed, mystery of God's becoming man in Christ.

The Doctrine of Salvation cont.

"I am thankful that I did not baptize any of you except Crispus and Gaius, so no one can say that you were baptized into my name.... For Christ did not send me to baptize, but to preach the gospel ..." (1 Cor. 1:14–15, 17).

"... we are baptized in order to obtain the remission of our sins" (Williams, *Bible Plan*, 11).

"... a man is justified by faith apart from observing the law" (Rom. 3:28).

"There are several things man must do in order to be saved. He must hear the gospel preached, he must repent, he must believe, he must obey God's Word, and *he must be baptized in Jesus name* [emphasis added]" (Clanton et al., *Salvation*, 119.)

"Baptism is *part of our spiritual circumcision* [emphasis original], or initiation into the new covenant (Colossians 2:11-13). Under the old covenant a male child officially received his name at his physical circumcision. (See Luke 2:21.) Water baptism is the time when our new family name is invoked upon us at our spiritual circumcision" (Bernard, *In the Name of Jesus*, 51).

"Is this blessedness only for the circumcised, or also for the uncircumcised? We have been saying that Abraham's faith was credited to him as righteousness. Under what circumstances was it credited? Was it after he was circumcised, or before? It was not after, but before! And he received the sign of circumcision, a seal of the righteousness that he had by faith while he was still uncircumcised" (Rom. 4:9–11).

"Water baptism is correctly administered by saying 'in the name of Jesus'" (Bernard, *Oneness of God*, 295).

"In later centuries, when attempts were made to teach a 'trinity' of persons in the Godhead, the baptismal formula was adapted to emphasize the three persons in a supposed 'trinity'" (Clanton et al., *Bible Doctrines*, 84).

"Therefore go and make disciples of all nations, baptizing them in the name of the Father and of the Son and of the Holy Spirit, and teaching them to obey everything I have commanded you" (Matt. 28:19–20).

"The baptism with, by, in, or of the Holy Ghost (Holy Spirit) is part of New Testament salvation, not an op-

"Again Jesus said, 'Peace be with you! As the Father has sent me, I am sending you.' And with that he breathed on

tional, postconversional experience (John 3:5; Romans 8:1–16; Ephesians 1:13–14; Titus 3:5)" (Bernard, *Essentials*, 19).

"Anyone who has never spoken in tongues has never been baptized with the Holy Ghost" (Reynolds, *Truth*, 53–4). (And if baptism with the Holy Spirit is "part of New Testament salvation" [Bernard, *Essentials*, 19], then whoever has not spoken in tongues is not saved.).

them [the disciples] and said, 'Receive the Holy Spirit'" (John 20:21–22).

"On one occasion, while he was eating with them, he [said to them]: '... in a few days you will be baptized with the Holy Spirit. ... But you will receive power when the Holy Spirit comes on you ...'" (Acts 1:4–5, 8).

"You, however, are controlled not by the sinful nature but by the Spirit, if the Spirit of God lives in you. ... And if the Spirit of him who raised Jesus from the dead is living in you, he who raised Christ from the dead will also give life to your mortal bodies through his Spirit, who lives in you" (Rom. 8:9, 11).

"And you also were included in Christ when you heard the word of truth, the gospel of your salvation. Having believed, you were marked in him with a seal, the promised Holy Spirit, who is a deposit guaranteeing our inheritance ..." (Eph. 1:13–14).

"Everyone who calls on the name of the Lord will be saved" (Rom. 10:13).

"Paul, ... to the church of God which is at Corinth, to those who have been sanctified in Christ Jesus, saints by calling, with all who in every place call upon the name of our Lord Jesus Christ... Now you are Christ's body, and individually members of it. And God has appointed in the church, first apostles, second prophets, third teachers, then miracles, then gifts of healings, helps, administrations, various kinds of tongues. All are not apostles, are they? ... All do not speak with tongues, do they?" (1 Cor. 1:1–2; 12:27–30,